Five Chiefs

FIVE CHIEFS

A Supreme Court Memoir

———◆———

John Paul Stevens

Little, Brown and Company

New York Boston London

Little, Brown and Company
Hachette Book Group
237 Park Avenue, New York, NY 10017
www.hachettebookgroup.com

First Edition: October 2011

Little, Brown and Company is a division of Hachette Book Group, Inc. The Little, Brown name and logo are trademarks of Hachette Book Group, Inc.

The publisher is not responsible for websites (or their content) that are not owned by the publisher.

Photo credits: p. 3, Copyright 1973. Photograph by Uldis Saule used by permission of Northwestern University School of Law; p. 9, 1883. By William Wetmore Story, Collection of the Supreme Court of the United States; p. 39, September 29, 2005. Photograph by Steven Petteway, Collection of the Supreme Court of the United States; p. 53, 1961. Oil on canvas by William F. Draper, Collection of the Supreme Court of the United States; p. 81, 1975. Oil on canvas by Charles J. Fox, Collection of the Supreme Court of the United States; p. 111, 1990. Oil on canvas by George Augusta, Collection of the Supreme Court of the United States; p. 167, 1994. Oil on canvas by Thomas Loepp, Collection of the Supreme Court of the United States; p. 201, October 31, 2005. Photograph by Steven Petteway, Collection of the Supreme Court of the United States; p. 229. Portrait in oil used with permission of James Ingwersen.

ISBN 978-0-316-19980-3
Library of Congress Control Number 2011934111

10 9 8 7 6 5 4 3 2 1

RRD-C

Printed in the United States of America

To my beautiful wife, Maryan, with thanks for keeping me healthy and happy

Contents

The world will little note, nor long remember, what we say here....

— *Abraham Lincoln, Gettysburg, Pennsylvania, November 19, 1863*

Five Chiefs

Introduction

Professor Nathaniel Nathanson sitting behind his desk and talking to an unidentified student at Northwestern University School of Law.

I T WAS IN THE fall of 1945, when I was a member of the entering class of freshmen at the Northwestern University School of Law, that I first met Nathaniel Nathanson, the professor who taught constitutional law. Nat was to have a profound influence on my understanding of the law during the ensuing years. His students sometimes referred to his class as "Nat's mystery hour" because he seemed to raise an endless number of questions but provided us with few solutions. He thought it more important to teach us how to find answers for ourselves than to indoctrinate us with his own views. A brilliant and lovable man, he inspired the affection and respect of the entire class. We were also impressed by the fact that in 1934 he had served as a law clerk to Justice Louis Brandeis, a jurist who was then — and still is — considered one of America's greatest judges.

In later years, events that were then unpredictable gave me a special reason for treating Brandeis as a hero. When Brandeis retired, in 1939, Justice William O. Douglas was selected to fill his vacancy, and after Justice Douglas set the record as the longest-serving justice in history — a record that still stands — he resigned in 1975, and President Ford nominated me to fill his vacancy. I like to think that I inherited not only Brandeis's seat but also some of his ideas and his respect for the law.

I well remember Nat's account of the culmination of his first assignment as a law clerk. Justice Brandeis had directed him to prepare a set of memos and deliver them to his home early in the morning. Instead of ringing the doorbell or knocking, he had been instructed, he should simply slip his work under the front door. He did so, and they were silently withdrawn from within. No conversation was necessary to ensure on-time delivery of future memos.

As a law clerk in 1934, Nat surely had personal contact with Charles Evans Hughes, then the chief justice, and with Associate Justice Harlan Fiske Stone, who would succeed Hughes as chief in 1941. I never set eyes on either of those chiefs, for I was still a first-year law student on April 22, 1946, when Stone suffered a fatal cerebral hemorrhage in open court.

President Harry Truman promptly nominated Fred Vinson — who had already served in all three branches of the federal government — to fill the vacancy. Vinson became the thirteenth chief justice of the United States — and the first with whom I would speak — on June 24, 1946. Over the years following my graduation from Northwestern in 1947, I had personal contact not only with Vinson but also with his four successors, Earl Warren, Warren Burger, William Rehnquist, and the Court's current leader, Chief Justice John Roberts.

My objective in writing this book is to share memories of these men and their work that may enable readers to receive insights similar to those that Nat conveyed to me six and a half decades ago. I do not intend to provide a comprehensive review of their jurisprudence or tenures. Instead, I hope that my recollections will improve public understanding of their work and the office that they each occupied with honor and varying degrees of expertise.

The chief justice of the United States has often been described as the "first among equals." He is "equal" because, like each of his eight colleagues, he has only one vote. It takes a majority of equally powerful votes to support a decision on the merits in any case before the Court. To achieve a desired outcome, the chief justice must convince as many colleagues to join him as must any other justice.

For that reason, as Byron White — who served as an active justice for thirty-one years — frequently observed, the confirmation of any new justice creates a new Court with significantly different dynamics than its predecessor. One could argue that 2010, when Elena Kagan joined the Court as its 112th justice, marked the inauguration of the Kagan Court rather than the continuation of the Roberts Court. If so, the Court that Lewis Powell and Bill Rehnquist joined in 1972 would be better termed the Powell-Rehnquist Court than the Burger Court.

But naming conventions are otherwise: Historians treat the story of our nation's more than one hundred different Courts as though it contained just seventeen chapters, each named after the chief justice whose tenure it tracks. In these memoirs I shall therefore include separate chapters discussing each of the five Courts during which I had some personal contact with the chief justice. Because the entire history of the Court includes only seventeen chapters, I begin with a brief review of the first twelve of those chapters. A full account of the tenure of each of the first twelve individuals who have presided over the Court could fill twelve books, but I will limit myself to a quick glimpse of each. I will then describe the unique duties of the officer whom Congress has described as the "Chief Justice of the United States." And, having served as the senior associate justice during my last fifteen years on the Court, I shall close with a few comments on the role of the person who might be dubbed the "second among equals." Because I shall refer to different provisions of the Constitution so frequently, I have included the entire text of that document in an appendix to this volume.

My reminiscences about Fred Vinson, Earl Warren, Warren Burger, Bill Rehnquist, and John Roberts make up the body of the book. For each of them, my memories primarily reflect a different point of view: that of another justice's law clerk for Vinson; of a practicing lawyer for Warren; of a circuit judge and junior justice for Burger; of a contemporary colleague for Rehnquist; and of an observer of superb advocacy before Roberts became a colleague. Because of those differing points of view, some autobiographical comments must be tolerated.

I

The First Twelve Chiefs

John Marshall, Chief Justice (1801–1835)

Bronze statue of Chief Justice John Marshall by William Wetmore Story. The
statue depicts Marshall seated in his judicial robe with his right hand outstretched
as if he were discussing the document curled up in his left hand.

ARTICLE III OF THE Constitution provides that the judicial power of the United States shall be vested in one Supreme Court and in such "inferior" courts as Congress shall from time to time ordain and establish. In 1789 Congress enacted the first Judiciary Act, which formally created a Supreme Court, composed of six judges, and a network of inferior courts. George Washington appointed all of the members of the Court who served during his two terms as president. Though the office of the chief justice has come to be perhaps the most exclusive of federal posts — only fourteen have been appointed since Washington left office, while forty-three chief executives have followed his tenure — Washington had the opportunity to appoint this nation's first three chief justices — John Jay, John Rutledge, and Oliver Ellsworth.

John Jay, who served from 1789 to 1795, was one of the authors of the Federalist Papers — the pamphlets that advocated ratification of the Constitution when they were written and that still provide guidance to judges interpreting that fundamental document today. Under Jay's leadership the Court rejected a request made by President Washington that it provide the executive branch with advisory opinions about the meanings of treaties, the laws of nations, and federal rules of law. In the Court's view, the Constitution drew lines separating the three departments of government, and that argued against having judges of the national court of last resort give advice to the executive. Jay's determination that advisory opinions would exceed the limits of the power to decide "cases and controversies" conferred on federal judges by Article III of the Constitution has been steadfastly followed throughout our history.

The most important case decided during Jay's tenure as chief was *Chisholm* v. *Georgia* (1793). The transaction that gave rise to the litigation occurred during the Revolutionary War: Georgia's purchase in 1777 of over $169,000 worth of supplies for troops quartered near Savannah. The South Carolina merchant who made the sale died before collecting the purchase price, but his executor — a man named Chisholm — filed suit against the State of Georgia to collect the debt. The question presented to the Supreme Court was whether a federal court had jurisdiction over a suit brought by a South Carolina resident against the sovereign State of Georgia.

By a vote of four to one, the five sitting justices concluded that the state was subject to suit in a federal forum. Each member of the Court wrote a separate opinion explaining his views. The majority necessarily held that jurisdiction had not only been conferred by Congress in the Judiciary Act but also was consistent with the provision in Article III extending federal judicial power to controversies "between a State and Citizens of another State." They rejected the argument that the English common-law doctrine of sovereign immunity provided the state with a defense to Chisholm's claim.

Justice James Iredell dissented. While he did not question Congress's power to change the common-law rule that prevented private citizens from suing unconsenting sovereigns, he did not believe that Congress had done so by enacting the Judiciary Act. Chief Justice Jay, however, addressed the more basic question — whether the common-law rule should exist in our newly formed government. In his opinion, he explained that in the democratic United States, there was no place for sovereign immunity. The doctrine was rooted in the feudal idea that the prince is the sovereign and that the people are merely his subjects. But in America, the people are sovereign. Unlike English subjects, "the citizens of America are equal as fellow citizens and as joint tenants in the sovereignty."

The *Chisholm* decision was not welcomed by states saddled with debts and threatened with insolvency. On February 20, 1793, two days after the Court decided the case, Massachusetts congressman Theodore Sedgwick proposed an amendment to the Constitution that would have deprived all federal courts of jurisdiction over any suit in which a state was named as a defendant. Instead of acting on that proposal, critics of *Chisholm* drafted, and two years later obtained ratification of, the Eleventh Amendment. That amendment eliminated the out-of-state residence of the plaintiff as a basis for federal jurisdiction in an action against a state, but it actually said nothing about the common-law doctrine of sovereign immunity. Nor did its text prohibit (or indeed even mention) suits brought against a state by its own citizens to enforce rights created by federal law. Nevertheless, as I shall explain in my chapter about Chief Justice Rehnquist, in later years it would provide the states with immunities that would have surprised John Jay.

In 1795, which happened to be the year the Eleventh

Amendment was ratified, John Jay resigned his position as chief justice to become governor of New York. President Washington nominated John Rutledge of South Carolina to replace him. While Rutledge had been a respected delegate to the Constitutional Convention in 1787, his career on the federal bench is noteworthy for its brevity.

In 1789, Rutledge had been one of Washington's first appointees to the Supreme Court. Although that appointment was confirmed by the Senate — as the Constitution requires for all Article III judges — Rutledge did not decide a case as a federal judge at that time because before he could do so, he chose instead to accept the position of chief justice of the South Carolina Supreme Court. When Jay resigned, in the summer of 1795, Washington named Rutledge to replace him by means of a recess appointment — a temporary appointment during which the appointee may serve in office without Senate approval. An unpopular speech, in which Rutledge criticized a treaty that John Jay had negotiated, plus concerns about his mental health persuaded the Senate to reject his nomination. History treats him as the second chief justice — and his portrait that hangs in the Court today assumes that he is entitled to that designation — but, as I shall explain in my chapter about Earl Warren, I am not persuaded that the president has the authority to confer judicial power on a nominee who has not been confirmed by the Senate. No more need be said about his tenure.

Oliver Ellsworth of Connecticut then became our third chief justice. He served from 1796 until his resignation took effect, on December 15, 1800. He had previously been both a delegate to the Constitutional Convention, where he made speeches favoring the abolition of slavery, and a United States senator. Perhaps his most notable contribution as chief justice was his initiation of the practice of having one justice write a single opinion explaining the Court's decision, replacing the custom followed in *Chisholm,* in which each of the justices expressed his individual views in a separate statement. Ever since, the Court has followed Ellsworth's practice whenever a majority can agree on the proper disposition of a case.

In 1775, before the Declaration of Independence was signed, nineteen-year-old John Marshall joined a group of Virginia militiamen that was called into action by Colonel Patrick Henry, commander of Virginia's provisional army, and engaged in combat with British troops. He served as an officer under George Washington at Valley Forge during the bitter winter of 1777–1778. His martial accomplishments were followed by distinguished work in the private practice of law, as a member of the Virginia convention that voted to ratify the Constitution, as a United States congressman from Virginia, and as a diplomat. While those credentials clearly qualified him to become our fourth chief justice, it was his work once in that office that made him our Court's greatest leader.

Appointed by John Adams in 1801, Marshall served until 1835. Decades after Marshall's death, Oliver Wendell Holmes — another universally lauded jurist and veteran of another foundational American war, that between the states — had this to say about Marshall: "If American law were to be represented by a single figure, skeptic and worshipper alike would agree without dispute that the figure could be one alone, and that one, John Marshall."

The quantity of Marshall's judicial output is impressive: he participated in over one thousand cases and authored more than five hundred Court opinions. But it is the quality of his work that commanded the admiration of his peers and successors. Most famous are his opinions in *Marbury* v. *Madison* (1803), *McCulloch* v. *Maryland* (1819), and *Gibbons* v. *Ogden* (1824).

Marbury was the first case in which the Court held an act of Congress to be unconstitutional. William Marbury had been named a justice of the peace in the final days of John Adams's presidency, his appointment had been confirmed by the Senate, and the secretary of state (who, not insignificantly, happened to be John Marshall — a fact that would have disqualified Marshall from participating in the case under today's recusal standards) had signed his commission — but had not delivered it — before Thomas Jefferson took office as the third president of the United States. When James Madison, the new secretary of state, refused to deliver the commission, Marbury filed a lawsuit in the United States Supreme Court invoking the Court's original jurisdiction and asking it to issue a writ of mandamus commanding Madison to do so. (*Mandamus* is an extraordinary writ that judges may use to order a defendant to perform a clear public duty when no other remedy is available.)

More than a year elapsed before Chief Justice Marshall announced his opinion for a unanimous Court. He concluded that Marbury had a right to receive his commission, and that the Judiciary Act enacted by Congress intended to give the Supreme

Court the authority to issue a writ of mandamus commanding Madison to deliver it. But then, in what might be described as a surprise ending, he concluded that the statute authorizing the Court to issue the writ was unconstitutional. The case is famous primarily for establishing the Court's authority to declare an act of Congress unconstitutional. For me, the case has always been puzzling because I have never found satisfying Marshall's explication of why the statute was unconstitutional.

He quite correctly identified a distinction of constitutional magnitude between cases, like Marbury's, that invoke the Court's original jurisdiction — that is, its jurisdiction to hear cases filed for the first time in the Supreme Court — and those invoking its appellate jurisdiction to review cases that had first been filed in a lower court. Unless Marbury's suit properly invoked the Court's original jurisdiction, the Court could not provide him with a remedy. While Article III of the Constitution authorizes original Supreme Court jurisdiction over any action against "public Ministers," Marshall might reasonably have construed that phrase to refer only to foreign ministers and not to the American secretary of state. But instead of holding that the Court could not grant relief against Madison for that reason, Marshall stated that the Court could not issue a mandamus in Marbury's case unless doing so could be characterized as an exercise of the Court's appellate jurisdiction.

I have never understood why that premise led him to the conclusion that the statute that Congress had enacted was unconstitutional. Why would the statute not have been perfectly valid in cases in which the Court properly had original jurisdiction, such as a suit by a foreign ambassador seeking relief against the secretary of state? I suppose I should have figured out the answer to this puzzlement during my many sessions in Nat's mystery hour.

There is nothing mysterious about Marshall's opinions in *McCulloch* and *Gibbons.* In *McCulloch,* the Court upheld the power of Congress to establish a national bank and invalidated an attempt by the State of Maryland to tax the business of the bank. The first holding rested on an interpretation of the last paragraph of Article I, Section 8 of the Constitution, which provides that in addition to the specific powers enumerated in that section, Congress may "make all Laws which shall be necessary and proper for carrying into Execution the foregoing Powers." Prior to the Constitution, Marshall recalled, the states had been bound together solely by the Articles of Confederation, which extended only limited powers to the Continental Congress that then served as the national legislature. By contrast, Marshall famously wrote, the Constitution provided the federal government with much broader powers: "Let the end be legitimate, let it be within the scope of the constitution, and all means which are appropriate, which are plainly adapted to that end, which are not prohibited, but consist with the letter and spirit of the constitution, are constitutional." The second conclusion — that Maryland could not tax the operations of the national bank — rested on what Marshall characterized as the "great principle" that "the constitution and laws made in pursuance thereof are supreme; that they control the constitution and laws of the respective States, and cannot be controlled by them." Because a state tax had the power to destroy a federal institution — in that case, the bank of the United States — the state tax had to give way.

The principle of federal supremacy also animated the *Gibbons* case. After receiving a federal license to engage in coastal trade, Thomas Gibbons sought to operate a steamboat service in the waters between Elizabethtown, New Jersey, and New York City. In an attempt to enforce monopoly privileges that the state had granted to Aaron Ogden, a New York court enjoined Gibbons's activities. In his opinion for the Court, Marshall held that Gibbons's federal license entitled him to an exemption from the New York laws. The opinion played an important role in the later development of rules that protect interstate commerce from burdens imposed by state laws even when Congress has not enacted any federal laws dealing specifically with the matter. (Cases that invalidate state laws that discriminate against out-of-state firms and thereby impede interstate commerce are often described as resting upon the "dormant" aspect of the commerce clause.)

While not as well known as *Marbury, McCulloch,* and *Gibbons,* Marshall's opinion in *Barron ex rel. Tiernan* v. *Mayor of Baltimore* (1833) merits mention because it provided the answer to an important question about the original meaning of the first eight amendments to the Constitution, commonly described as the Bill of Rights. Marshall held that those amendments limit the powers of the federal government but place no limitations on the powers of the state governments.

Under that view, the Second Amendment's protection of the right to keep and bear arms would prohibit Congress from interfering with a state's regulation of its own militia but would allow the states complete freedom to regulate the possession and use of weapons. As a result, prior to the adoption of the Fourteenth

Amendment, after the Civil War, individual citizens had to rely entirely on their own state constitutions as the sole source of protection against arbitrary state action.

Our fifth chief justice, Roger Taney, was appointed to that office by President Andrew Jackson in 1836 and served until his death, in 1864. He was the author of the majority opinion in the Dred Scott case — *Dred Scott* v. *Sandford* (1857) — which held that a slave did not become free when taken into a free state, that Congress could not bar slavery in a territory, and that African Americans could not be citizens of the United States or — for constitutional purposes — of their own states. The only good thing that can be said about that case is that Abraham Lincoln's criticism of it in his famous debates with Stephen Douglas received nationwide attention and helped get him elected president of the United States.

In 1864, President Lincoln selected Salmon P. Chase, a former rival in the 1860 presidential election and later Lincoln's secretary of the treasury, to become the sixth "Chief Justice of the Supreme Court of the United States." Perhaps motivated by the hope that he would one day be elected president, Chase assumed the more imposing title of "Chief Justice of the United States," a title that Congress began to use in subsequent legislation and that has been used by all of Chase's successors.

Like his immediate predecessor, Chase may be best known for his involvement in a dispute that arose out of the divisive legacy of slavery in the United States: He presided over the impeachment trial of President Andrew Johnson. In the wake of the Civil War and the assassination of President Lincoln, Johnson clashed repeatedly with the Republican majority in Congress, often over matters of race and Reconstruction. To protect the man Lincoln had appointed secretary of war (Edwin Stanton) from removal by Johnson, Congress passed the Tenure of Office Act, which required the president to obtain the consent of the Senate before making such a removal. When Johnson effectively defied Congress by removing Stanton without Senate consent, the House of Representatives impeached him, launching a Senate trial to determine whether he would be removed from office. There, Johnson contended that he had not technically violated the Tenure of Office Act because it protected officials only during the tenure of the president who appointed them. Once Lincoln died, Johnson argued, the act ceased to apply to Stanton. While Johnson failed to convince a majority of senators to take his side, his opponents could muster only thirty-five of the fifty-four available votes, one vote short of the "Concurrence of two thirds of the Members present" required for conviction by Article I, Section 3, paragraph 6 of the Constitution.

After Chase died, in 1873, President Ulysses Grant considered several potential successors, vacillated for six months, and finally nominated the successful Ohio lawyer Morrison Waite to become the seventh chief. Waite's fourteen-year tenure is notable for two quite different reasons: It illustrates the heavy burden that work on the Court then entailed. And it encompasses decisions severely limiting federal protections for newly freed slaves that the framers of the Fourteenth Amendment had sought to provide.

While Waite was the chief, the Court decided 3,470 cases. Waite wrote 872 of the opinions disposing of those cases, a number that attests to the important role he played in efficiently discharging the Court's responsibilities. He joined significant opinions written by colleagues construing the equal protection clause of the Fourteenth Amendment to prohibit the exclusion of African Americans from juries in criminal trials and protecting Chinese residents of San Francisco from discriminatory enforcement of an ordinance regulating laundries. But his own most significant opinion in the area — *United States* v. *Cruikshank* (1876) — can only be described as a disaster.

In the infamous Colfax massacre in Louisiana on Easter Sunday 1873, dozens of blacks were slaughtered by a band of white men, one of whom was William Cruikshank. Because state authorities did not punish the men for murder or any other state offense, the federal government indicted them for violating a statute enacted by Congress in 1870 that prohibited two or more persons from banding together to deprive their victims of rights protected by the federal Constitution. According to the indictment the defendants had intentionally deprived their victims of several federal rights, including the right to peaceable assembly protected by the First Amendment, the right to keep and bear arms protected by the Second Amendment, and the right to life and liberty protected by the Fourteenth Amendment. Cruikshank and two of his confederates were convicted in federal court, but the Supreme Court reversed. As Waite reasoned for the Court, the First and Second Amendment rights that the murderers had been convicted of violating merely limited the powers of the federal government, and the Fourteenth Amendment merely limited the powers of the states; none of the amendments prohibited the individual acts committed by the defendants. The unfortunate decision paved the way for continued racial violence and the enactment of state laws throughout the South that deprived blacks of full citizenship for decades.

Melville Fuller had been practicing law in Chicago for over thirty years when President Grover Cleveland selected him as our eighth chief. He initiated what I regard as an extremely important custom that all members of the Court still follow today. Before the beginning of an oral argument session, usually while donning his or her black robe, each justice greets every colleague with a handshake. That brief greeting confirms not only the personal friendships that all members of the Court share but also the more fundamental point that our common goals outweigh our individual differences.

I do not know how many other courts follow that practice, though I can attest that such handshakes are not unique to the Supreme Court. I still remember the warmth of the greeting that Luther Swygert and Roger Kiley, two federal circuit judges appointed by a Democratic president, extended to their new Republican colleague before I went on the bench at the Seventh Circuit Court of Appeals in the fall of 1970 to hear my first oral argument. Past political differences become entirely irrelevant when a federal judge goes to work.

While Fuller was the chief, Congress enacted the Judiciary

Act of 1891, which led to a significant decrease in the workload of the Supreme Court. The statute created a new layer of intermediate appellate courts, known as circuit courts of appeals, that came to handle most of the appeals from decisions of federal trial courts. As an example, the statute authorized the Court of Appeals for the Seventh Circuit (where I served from 1970 to 1975) to hear appeals from each of the federal trial courts in Wisconsin, Illinois, and Indiana. As a consequence of that important change, many of the appeals that had previously gone directly to the Supreme Court were addressed first — and often only — by the circuit courts.

Though its workload was diminished, the Court continued to hear four important categories of cases. First, while the statute eliminated the losing parties' right to take an appeal to the Supreme Court in many federal cases, it gave them the right to file petitions for certiorari, often referred to as "certs." As a matter of settled practice, if four justices are persuaded that a particular case merits further review and vote to grant cert, the Court will hear the case. Over the course of the twentieth century, these cases came to dominate the Supreme Court's docket. Second, there is a category of cases — today relatively small — in which Congress has given the losing party a right to a direct Supreme Court review of federal trial court decisions. This so-called mandatory jurisdiction of the Court has changed from time to time since 1891. Cases challenging the constitutionality of campaign finance laws are an example. The appellant in such a case files a document known as a jurisdictional statement. Third, the Court has always had jurisdiction to review certain state supreme court decisions denying a litigant's claim that his federal rights have been violated. Fourth, the Court's original jurisdiction as defined by Article III — which has been most frequently invoked in controversies between states over their boundaries or their rights in interstate waters — was not affected by the 1891 act.

Lochner v. *New York* (1905) was the most important case decided during Fuller's tenure as chief, which lasted from 1888 until 1910. A majority of five justices held that a New York statute prohibiting the employment of bakers for more than ten hours a day or sixty hours a week was unconstitutional because it interfered with the liberty of the employer and his employees to contract with one another. The case is famous because there is virtually universal agreement among judges and scholars that it was incorrectly decided. More important, it is the case in which Justice Oliver Wendell Holmes wrote the most influential dissenting opinion in the Court's history.

The case raised a basic question about the meaning of the word *liberty* as it is used in the due process clause of the Fourteenth Amendment, which declares that no state shall "deprive any person of life, liberty, or property, without due process of law." In a ten-page dissent joined by Justices Edward White and William Day, the first Justice John Harlan (grandfather of the second Justice John Harlan, whom President Dwight Eisenhower would appoint) explained in some detail why the statute was a reasonable regulation of liberty. Justice Holmes's solo dissent contained just two paragraphs.

In the first paragraph Holmes explained that "a constitution is not intended to embody a particular economic theory" and that the "accident of our finding certain opinions natural and familiar or novel and even shocking ought not to conclude our judgment upon the question whether statutes embodying them conflict with the Constitution of the United States." The second paragraph focused on the meaning of the word *liberty* without mentioning the justifications for the New York statute that the other dissenters had discussed at length. He wrote: "I think that the word liberty in the Fourteenth Amendment is perverted when it is held to prevent the natural outcome of a dominant opinion, unless it can be said that a rational and fair man necessarily would admit that the statute proposed would infringe fundamental principles as they have been understood by the traditions of our people and our law."

I grappled with the meaning of Holmes's dissent in one of the first cases that I confronted as a court of appeals judge: *Fitzgerald v. Porter Memorial Hospital* (1975). The case involved a claim by married couples that a hospital policy barring fathers from being present during the delivery of their babies deprived them of a substantive right protected by the Fourteenth Amendment. Before studying the case, I had assumed that the due process clause protects only a right to fair procedures before a state could deprive a citizen of life, liberty, or property — that that had been the real point of Holmes's *Lochner* dissent. But a more careful study convinced me that Holmes did believe the clause protects some substantive rights that judges must identify in particular cases. The case therefore required us to decide whether the word *liberty* in the Fourteenth Amendment encompassed the substantive right that the parents had asserted. My good friend and colleague

Judge Robert Sprecher was persuaded that it did. While I wrote the majority opinion concluding that the hospital regulation did not violate the Constitution, I was also convinced that the word *liberty* does protect some substantive rights that judges must identify in specific cases.

Edward White was the first sitting justice to be elevated to higher office. A Civil War veteran who had fought in the Confederate army, he was appointed to the Court in 1894 by President Grover Cleveland and, after serving as an associate justice for sixteen years, named chief justice by President William Howard Taft in 1910. He served until his death in 1921 and was succeeded by the president who had appointed him chief.

Despite having fought on opposite sides in the Civil War, White and Justice Holmes reportedly became warm friends with great respect for each other while on the Court. In 1911, during White's first year as chief justice, Holmes joined what have arguably become White's two most famous opinions for the Court: *Standard Oil Co.* v. *United States* and *United States* v. *American Tobacco Co.* In them, the Court held that the combinations of former competitors in holding companies formed, respectively, by the Standard Oil Company and the American Tobacco Company violated the Sherman antitrust law. In reaching that result, White discussed at length the so-called rule of reason — the rule stating that only acts that unreasonably restrain trade violate federal antitrust laws.

As I explained in an opinion written shortly after I joined the Court, it was necessary to adopt such a rule because a literal reading of the text of the Sherman Act would have outlawed the entire body of private contract law. White's opinions, coupled with an opinion by Charles Evans Hughes, a colleague of his who would later become the eleventh chief justice, broadly construed the commerce clause of the Constitution to authorize federal regulation of business activities that affect interstate commerce as well as activities that actually involve interstate transactions.

As was true of his predecessor, the most significant opinion announced during White's tenure as chief was written by another justice. It was Justice Peckham who authored the Court's opinion in *Ex parte Young* (1908), which rejected Minnesota's sovereign immunity defense to a suit brought by a shareholder of a railroad claiming that newly enacted Minnesota statutes regulating railroad rates violated the federal Constitution. A federal district judge had entered an injunction against Young, the attorney general of Minnesota, forbidding him from enforcing the statutes. When the attorney general had nonetheless enforced the state law, the federal district judge had threatened to commit Young to federal custody for violating the injunction. Young then asked the U.S. Supreme Court to issue a writ of habeas corpus ending any such confinement. He argued that the Eleventh Amendment deprived the federal district court of jurisdiction to enjoin him from performing his official duties. The Court rejected his defense.

In an opinion joined by all his colleagues except Justice Harlan, Justice Peckham reasoned that because an unconstitutional state law is "void," a state official who attempts to enforce such a law is acting as an individual rather than as a state official. The state, he reasoned, had no power to grant such a person "any immunity from responsibility to the supreme authority of the United States."

The tenth chief justice, William Howard Taft, was one of the two top students in his class when he graduated from Yale in 1878. He became a member of the Yale Law School faculty after the end of his term as president of the United States. Before his election to the presidency, in 1908, he served as a federal judge on the Sixth Circuit Court of Appeals. In 1921, after being nominated by President Warren G. Harding, he became the first chief justice to have previously served as the judge of an inferior federal court. That fact is particularly remarkable because all but one of the current members of the Court are former federal circuit judges, and the one exception — Justice Kagan — had former federal judicial experience when she served as a law clerk to Justice Thurgood Marshall, in 1987. (She had also previously been solicitor general — often referred to as the tenth Supreme Court justice — and had been nominated, though not confirmed, for the seat on the U.S. Court of Appeals for the D.C. Circuit that future Chief Justice John Roberts came to occupy.)

As our tenth chief justice, Taft is entitled to the credit for two important changes in the work of the Court. He persuaded Congress to adopt the Judiciary Act of 1925, which reduced the categories of cases in which the Supreme Court must hear every appeal, and he argued successfully for the construction of the beautiful building located just east of the Capitol, where the Court is now located.

Before the completion of our "marble palace," in 1935, the justices met in several locations within the Capitol. From 1810 to

1860, the justices convened in a small, windowless, but attractive courtroom designed by Benjamin Latrobe. The architect of the Capitol has preserved this courtroom, now known as the Old Supreme Court Chamber, and before presidential inaugurations, the justices meet in that historic courtroom to don their robes. In 1860, the Court moved into the Senate's original chamber, now known as the Old Senate Chamber, which the Senate had that year outgrown with the admission of new states into the Union. But the justices did not have individual offices in the Capitol. Indeed, until 1935, the justices did most of their work at their homes — which is why Nat Nathanson delivered his first memos to Justice Brandeis by slipping them under his front door. Chief Justice Taft correctly concluded that they could work more efficiently in new quarters. He was also correct in thinking that the practice of arguing judicial cases in the Capitol was somewhat inconsistent with the constitutional separation of the powers of the three branches of government. Unfortunately, Taft died in 1930 before the magnificent building the Court now occupies was completed.

It was during Taft's tenure that Justice James McReynolds, often considered a reactionary, wrote two important opinions broadly interpreting the term *liberty* as used in the Fourteenth Amendment. In *Meyer* v. *Nebraska* (1923), the Court overturned Robert Meyer's conviction for teaching the German language to high school students. In *Pierce* v. *Society of Sisters* (1925), the Court sustained a challenge by parochial and private schools to an Oregon statute requiring children to attend public schools. In both cases, the Court held that the state laws in question were invalid as they were deprivations of liberty protected by the due process clause of the Fourteenth Amendment.

Justice Brandeis built on these and other similar decisions involving the meaning of the word *liberty* in his concurrence in a 1927 free-speech case known as *Whitney* v. *California*. It was his reasoning concerning the existence and importance of the substantive content of the due process clause that qualifies his opinion as the most significant one released during Taft's tenure as chief justice. I shall quote an excerpt:

> Despite arguments to the contrary which had seemed to me persuasive, it is settled that the due process clause of the Fourteenth Amendment applies to matters of substantive law as well as to matters of procedure. Thus all fundamental rights comprised within the term liberty are protected by the Federal Constitution from invasion by the States. The right of free speech, the right to teach and the right of assembly are, of course, fundamental rights.... These may not be denied or abridged.... Those who won our independence believed that the final end of the State was to make men free to develop their faculties; and that in its government the deliberative forces should prevail over the arbitrary. They valued liberty both as an end and as a means. They believed liberty to be the secret of happiness and courage to be the secret of liberty.

In 1910, well before becoming chief justice and while still president of the United States, Taft nominated Charles Evans Hughes to be an associate justice. Six years later Hughes became the Republican candidate for president and resigned from the Court; he was narrowly defeated by Woodrow Wilson. Hughes served as secretary of state under Presidents Harding and Coolidge, and in 1930, when Taft retired, President Hoover nominated him to the position of chief justice. During both of his periods of service on the Court, he was regarded as a brilliant lawyer and an especially able jurist. I am sure that Bill Rehnquist thought of him as the predecessor whom he most wanted to emulate.

Hughes's tenure as chief began during the Great Depression and included the first two terms of Franklin Delano Roosevelt's presidency. Immediately after FDR took office, Congress enacted a number of far-reaching statutes, several of which the Supreme Court declared unconstitutional. Hughes wrote the Court opinion in *A.L.A. Schechter Poultry Corp.* v. *United States* (1935), which held the National Industrial Recovery Act of 1933 — a major piece of FDR's economic program — unconstitutional. But he dissented in other cases striking down laws that FDR had championed.

The Court's decisions during the first few years of the New Deal created what FDR regarded as a constitutional crisis. In 1937, Roosevelt responded by proposing a Court-packing plan that would have enabled him to enlarge the Court by appointing as many additional justices as the number then on the Court who had served for at least ten years and were at least seventy years old, provided that the total membership did not exceed fifteen. Presumably, the fifteen-justice limit was chosen because six members of the Court were over seventy.

In his message to Congress supporting the proposal, the president argued that the Court was behind in its work and implied that judges over seventy were so "aged and infirm" that they could not carry their share of the load. Hughes did not then — and I do not now — find that argument persuasive. In March, he responded with a letter to the chairman of the Senate Judiciary Committee explaining that the Court was fully abreast of its work and that in his opinion an increase in the number of justices would impair its efficiency. In June, the Judiciary Committee issued its report recommending rejection of the proposal as a "needless, futile, and utterly dangerous abandonment of constitutional principle."

Shortly before that report was issued, Hughes announced his opinion for the Court upholding the constitutionality of a major piece of economic legislation that Roosevelt had lobbied hard to have enacted: the National Labor Relations Act. That decision suggested that the constitutional crisis that precipitated the Court-packing plan was not as severe as FDR believed.

In that same year Hughes assigned an important opinion dealing with the meaning of the word *liberty* in the Fourteenth Amendment to Benjamin Cardozo, a justice who had been appointed by President Herbert Hoover after a career on the New York Court of Appeals that had earned him a reputation as one of the country's most learned and eloquent judges. In *Palko* v. *Connecticut* (1937), the Court held that a statute permitting the prosecutor to take an appeal to a state appellate court from a judgment of not guilty in a criminal case was constitutional, even though the double jeopardy clause of the Fifth Amendment would have prohibited a similar appeal in a federal case. It rejected the argument that the Fourteenth Amendment made every provision of the Bill of Rights that limits the power of the federal government a limit on state power as well. Instead, in Justice Cardozo's words, it was only the particular amendments that "have been found to be implicit in the concept of ordered liberty" that were applicable to the states. In a series of later cases, the Court decided that most provisions of the Bill of Rights do apply to the states, but it has never incorporated them all en masse.

Hughes continued to perform exemplary judicial work at the head of a nine-justice Court until his retirement, in 1941.

Harlan F. Stone, our twelfth chief justice, was a scholar. He received a Phi Beta Kappa key when he graduated in 1894 from Amherst College, where Calvin Coolidge was a classmate. Stone next studied and then taught law at Columbia Law School; he began a thirteen-year stint as dean there in 1910. In the fall of 1922 he taught the course in personal property to a class that included William O. Douglas, who would later become a colleague on the Supreme Court. A year later he left Columbia to become a partner in a New York law firm. Coolidge, now president, then made him attorney general and, a year later, an associate justice of the Supreme Court. In 1941, after sixteen years as an associate justice, he was named chief justice by President Franklin Roosevelt.

As an associate justice, Stone often joined Hughes, Brandeis, and Benjamin Cardozo in dissents from decisions striking down New Deal legislation. There, as well as in majority opinions written when he was the chief, he interpreted the commerce clause broadly, as John Marshall had in his *Gibbons* opinion. A characteristic example was his opinion for a unanimous Court in *United States* v. *California* (1936), which held that Congress's "plenary power to regulate commerce" applied equally to commercial activities of states and private individuals: "The state can no more deny the power if its exercise has been authorized by Congress than can an individual." (Years later, in an opinion that was destined to be overruled, Justice Rehnquist characterized that statement as "simply wrong"; see *National League of Cities* v. *Usery* [1976].)

Two of Stone's many fine opinions merit special comment. In *Minersville School Dist.* v. *Gobitis* (1940), he alone dissented from the Court's decision that two young children could be expelled from a public school because their unique religious beliefs made it impossible for them to salute the flag in conformance with district policy. He thought the majority's reasoning inconsistent with earlier cases stressing "the importance of a searching judicial inquiry into the legislative judgment in situations where prejudice against discrete and insular minorities may tend to curtail the operation of those political processes ordinarily to be relied on to protect minorities." The dissent is especially remarkable because in a similar case that was decided only three years later, the Court overruled the *Gobitis* case. Three of the justices who had joined the majority in that case — Black, Douglas, and Murphy — acknowledged that they had been mistaken and joined the overruling opinion written by Justice Jackson.

Chief Justice Stone's dissent in *Girouard* v. *United States* (1946) also arose out of an individual's conscientious objection to a governmental requirement. Although willing to take an oath of allegiance to the United States in order to become a citizen, Girouard was unable to swear that he would take up arms in support of the country. The question was whether he could nevertheless qualify for citizenship. In earlier cases presenting the same issue,

Stone had joined dissents from decisions holding that the applicant could not qualify for citizenship without taking the required oath. In the *Girouard* case, the majority decided to overrule those cases and adopt the views that Stone had previously endorsed. Stone, however, thought that the legislative history of proposed amendments to the statute that Congress had refused to enact demonstrated that Congress had rejected his interpretation. Although he still thought the law unwise, he believed he had a duty to accept what he understood to be the interpretation that Congress intended.

Stone planned to explain his views in an oral announcement of his dissent in open court, but while Justice Douglas was reading the majority opinion, Stone suffered his fatal cerebral hemorrhage.

Stone was unquestionably a great jurist and a great American. There were, however, two imperfections in his career that must be acknowledged. Though a thorough and brilliant scholar, he was an exceptionally poor presiding officer during the Court's deliberations in conference, which sometimes consumed more than two days. And his two most significant wartime opinions — *Ex parte Quirin,* rejecting challenges to their death sentences by putative German saboteurs who had voluntarily surrendered to the FBI, and *In re Yamashita,* upholding a military tribunal's death sentence imposed on a Japanese general because of atrocities committed by soldiers under his command — may have bent the rule of law in response to perceived military necessity. As Justice Antonin Scalia correctly observed of *Ex parte Quirin* in his fine dissenting opinion in *Hamdi* v. *Rumsfeld* (2004), "The [*Quirin*] case was not this Court's finest hour." And as my former boss

Wiley Rutledge explained at length in his dissenting opinion, the Japanese general in *Yamashita* did not receive a fair trial.

As a postscript to my brief comments about the first twelve leaders of the Supreme Court, I should add my opinion that five chiefs stand out as national leaders entitled to our highest respect: John Jay, John Marshall, William Howard Taft, Charles Evans Hughes, and Harlan F. Stone. I shall not try to answer the question whether all, or any, of the five chiefs I have known merit similar respect, but I hope the ensuing recollections may help others do so.

II

Chief Justice of the United States

Chief Justice John G. Roberts Jr. is sworn in by Justice John Paul Stevens at the White House. Left to right: President George W. Bush, Chief Justice Roberts, Jane Sullivan Roberts, and Justice Stevens.

ARTICLE II OF THE Constitution imposes at least three conditions on aspirants to the office of president of the United States. He or she must be a "natural born Citizen, or a Citizen of the United States, at the time of the Adoption of this Constitution,...attained to the Age of thirty-five Years, and been fourteen Years a Resident within the United States." If these citizenship requirements were taken literally, to become president today, an individual would have to have been a citizen "at the time of the adoption of this Constitution" (that is, in 1788). I am confident that the framers did not expect us to adopt a literal interpretation of those words.

But whether the Constitution intended to impose three qualifications or four for the president, it imposes none at all for the chief justice. The Constitution mentions the office but does not require that its occupant be a citizen, a lawyer, a voter, or even an adult. Article I mandates that "the Chief Justice shall preside" at any trial by the Senate of an impeachment of the president of the United States, but the office is not otherwise mentioned. And Article III protects the tenure and compensation of "Judges, both of the supreme and inferior Courts," but without any special reference to the chief. Outside the context of impeachments, then, the Constitution treats all judges of the Supreme Court as equals.

In practice, however, the chief justice is the first among these equals. Congress has recognized and legislated as much. One is not merely the chief justice of the Supreme Court but, as a matter of statute, "Chief Justice of the United States." The chief justice receives a higher salary than an associate justice and has statutory duties that no other judge performs. In 1789, Congress appropriated five hundred dollars per year as compensation for the chief's extra labors, an amount that may have been fair at the time. It is less clear that when Fred Vinson became chief justice, more than a century and a half later, his annual salary of $25,500 fairly compensated him for his additional duties in light of the $25,000 each that other members of the Court received. Nonetheless, the amount of the bonus that the chief justice received remained the same until Warren Burger succeeded Earl Warren in 1969.

The relative value of the chief justice's extra work has risen somewhat in intervening years. Chief Justice Roberts is now paid $223,500, nearly $10,000 more than the $213,900 that each of his colleagues receives. The comparative figures demonstrate that Congress assigns a much higher value to the judicial duties that all members of the Court share equally than it does to those unique to the chief. If their pay is the measure, then the nine justices are 96 percent equal, and the chief's work differs by only 4 percent from that of his colleagues. In my judgment all federal judges are underpaid, but none more so than the chief.

The chores for which the chief receives some 96 percent of his compensation are similar to those performed by each of his eight colleagues. The work of the entire Court generally falls into three categories: choosing which cases to decide; deciding those cases; and explaining those decisions. The cases that the Court is asked to decide are extremely numerous. Most of them are initiated by the filing of a petition for certiorari, which, as noted earlier, is a request for the Supreme Court to review a decision made by a federal court of appeals or the highest appellate court in a state. It takes four justices to grant such a petition; well over 98 percent of requests are denied unanimously.

After deciding whether to hear a case initiated by a cert petition, the Court usually enters a simple order granting or denying the petition; the order expresses no view about the merits of the lower court's decision. Jurisdictional statements, it will be recalled, also initiate some of the cases that the Court is asked to decide. The Court may respond to such statements in several different ways. Most frequently it will enter an order noting probable jurisdiction, which means that the parties will then file written briefs and present an oral argument to the Court. If the case raises a substantial question but the Court is uncertain about its jurisdiction, it may enter a postpone order, which directs the parties to include in their briefs a discussion of the case's jurisdictional issue as well as its merits. If the Court concludes that there is no merit to the appeal and that it should dispose of the case without further argument, it will enter one of three orders: in cases coming from state courts, it will simply affirm without further explanation; in cases coming from federal courts, it will either dismiss for want of jurisdiction, which means that no federal statute has authorized the Court to hear the case, or dismiss for want of a substantial federal question, which means that the case involves no significant issue of federal law. The vast majority of the papers filed in the Court relate to its function of choosing which cases to decide.

After a cert petition is granted or the Court has noted probable jurisdiction of an appeal, the parties file written briefs, and an oral argument is held. Thereafter, in a conference attended only by the justices, the members of the Court discuss and vote on how the case should be decided. Usually, but not always, the decision made at conference determines the outcome.

After the conference, the senior justice in the majority — most often the chief — assigns either himself or another justice in the majority the task of writing an opinion explaining the result. The author then prepares a draft that is circulated to all members of the Court. After receiving this draft, each justice suggests changes, prepares a dissent or a separate concurring opinion, or simply joins the circulating draft. Depending on the difficulty of the case, the process of explaining the decision may take days, weeks, or months. On rare occasions, the Court is unable to resolve all the issues in a case before the term ends (usually in late June or the first week in July) and orders the parties to file additional briefs and present a second oral argument in the next term, which, following a long tradition, begins on the first Monday in October.

The duties for which the chief justice receives only 4 percent of his pay are weighty and numerous. Some are well known. By tradition, the chief justice administers the oath of office to the president on Inauguration Day; presides over proceedings in open court and in the confidential conferences attended by only the nine justices; and, in most cases, assigns the writing of the opinions that explain why litigants have won or lost their cases. (When the chief is in dissent, the senior justice in the majority makes the assignment.)

Congress has enacted a number of special statutory provisions giving the chief the authority to designate federal judges and retired justices to serve in different capacities in the federal judicial system. For example, he selects the judges who serve on the seven-member judicial panel on multidistrict litigation as well as the eleven district judges of the Foreign Intelligence Surveillance Court, who decide whether to grant applications to engage in electronic surveillance for national security purposes. There are more bureaucratic responsibilities as well: A separate group of statutes requires his participation in the process of relieving lower court chief judges of their duties as chiefs while retaining their active status as judges. One of those statutes provides him with authority to sign a certificate of disability to be presented to the president when either an associate justice or a lower court judge seeks to retire on account of disability.

The chief also serves as the circuit justice for three of the thirteen United States Courts of Appeals. Each member of the Court serves as the circuit justice for at least one circuit, ruling on such matters as extensions of time in which to file briefs and emergency applications to grant stays delaying the enforcement of orders entered by federal judges in the circuit. For most such applications, the decision of the circuit justice is final. But in some cases, such as requests to postpone the execution of a prison inmate on death row, the circuit justice will refer the application to the entire Court for decision. In these instances, the circuit justice prepares a memorandum setting forth his or her views about how to respond to the application. A majority vote will then determine whether to accept the circuit justice's recommendation.

Following the tradition established by John Marshall, the chief's portfolio includes the court sitting in Richmond, Virginia, which today makes him circuit justice for the Fourth

Circuit. That circuit encompasses Maryland, North Carolina, South Carolina, Virginia, and West Virginia. He is also circuit justice for the District of Columbia Court of Appeals, which reviews decisions of federal district courts in the District of Columbia as well as a variety of decisions by federal agencies, and for the Court of Appeals for the Federal Circuit. The Federal Circuit hears appeals from all over the country, though only on certain subjects, those which, broadly speaking, include claims against the United States, patents, and cases involving international trade or American Indians.

Among the chief justice's most important responsibilities is presiding over the Judicial Conference of the United States. This body, which was conceived by Chief Justice Taft and later authorized by an act of Congress, is the policy-making body for the federal judiciary. Its twenty-six members consist of the chief judge of each of the thirteen courts of appeals and one district judge from each of those circuits. In his role as presiding officer, the chief prepares the agenda and appoints committees that recommend improvements in the administration of justice in the federal courts. There are currently twenty-five committees that address a broad range of issues, including case administration and management, codes of conduct, court space and facilities, and rules of procedure. The statutes creating the Judicial Conference require the conference, which in practice means its presiding officer, to submit to Congress an annual report of its proceedings and its recommendations for legislation. The chief justice also chairs the board of the Federal Judicial Center. The FJC provides continuing education for federal judges, including orientation programs for new judges, and conducts empirical research on court-related issues, such as management and operations, for both the Judicial Conference and Congress.

The chief also approves the participation of retired Supreme Court justices in the work of other federal courts. Justice David Souter, who retired on June 29, 2009 (exactly a year before I did), has served regularly in the First Circuit, the jurisdiction of which includes his home state of New Hampshire, while Sandra Day O'Connor, who retired on January 31, 2006, has visited most, if not all, of the courts of appeals.

After Tom Clark retired, in 1967, when his son, Ramsey, became the attorney general, he tried cases as a district judge and helped out in the appellate courts. In one of those cases, my partner Bill Myers and I represented Charles O. Finley, who had just moved his American League baseball team from Kansas City, Missouri, to Oakland, California. Years earlier, the team had been located in Philadelphia, where Connie Mack had entered into a long-term contract guaranteeing that the team's concessionaire would retain its rights if the team should move. Justice Clark not only refused to enforce the terms of that contract but also awarded damages to Finley in his counterclaim against the concessionaire. (The case had a longer life span than my career on the court of appeals; although I was active in the case for over three years, Bill was unable to bring it to a successful conclusion until months after I joined the Supreme Court.)

Two highly publicized cases decided by the Court of Appeals for the Seventh Circuit while I was a member illustrate the importance of a unique responsibility that the chief justice must occasionally exercise: his duty to select a judge from one district to preside at a trial if all the active judges in that district are disqualified and to select a panel of appellate judges if all the appellate judges in that circuit are disqualified. One of those cases, *United States* v. *Dellinger* — popularly known as the conspiracy seven case — arose out of the demonstrations in Chicago's Grant Park during the 1968 Democratic Convention. Those demonstrations lasted for several days, included an attempted march to the convention site, and resulted in hundreds of injuries to and multiple indictments of both protesters and police. The trial of the protesters went on for months, producing a mammoth record and a number of highly controversial rulings by district judge Julius Hoffman. Because of the importance of the case and the size of the record, the court of appeals decided that the members of the three-judge panel reviewing the decisions — Judges Tom Fairchild, Walter Cummings, and Wilbur Pell, who had been chosen by lot — should not participate in any other cases until after *Dellinger* had been argued and decided. The panel reversed Judge Hoffman and sent the case back for another trial before a different judge, and Chief Justice Burger appointed Judge Edward Gignoux of the District of Maine to preside over those proceedings.

While the court of appeals was undermanned because three judges were preoccupied with the conspiracy seven appeal, another active judge, Otto Kerner Jr., was indicted by a federal grand jury for conduct that had occurred while he was governor of Illinois. Warren Burger designated Robert Taylor, a district judge for the Eastern District of Tennessee, to preside at the trial in Chicago. Burger also appointed the special panel of circuit judges who heard Kerner's appeal and affirmed his conviction.

Moreover, because only four active judges — Swygert, Kiley, Sprecher, and myself — were available to process a volume of cases that was considered a heavy workload for even the normal complement of eight judges, it was necessary to invite judges from other federal courts to sit with us on a regular basis. All of those special invitations required the approval of the chief justice.

Burger's approval of those requests provided me with the opportunity to form a close friendship with Justice Tom Clark, who was the most frequent visiting judge. When I appeared before Justice Clark in the Finley case, I respected him as an extremely competent jurist with excellent taste in bow ties. That respect grew into a real friendship when we were colleagues — albeit only temporarily — on the court of appeals. He always insisted on taking the most burdensome writing assignments, explaining that that was how he could be most helpful to us. As a retired justice, Tom did almost as much judicial work as he had as an active justice. I shall never forget Tom's selfless and invaluable contribution during that particularly difficult period.

In addition to administering the oath of office to the president on Inauguration Day, the chief justice customarily administers two oaths to each of his new colleagues. When I was sworn in, in 1975, I was told that the first (the so-called constitutional oath) entitles the new justice to exercise judicial power, and that the second (the statutory oath) entitles him or her to receive compensation. (I have since been advised that both oaths are necessary for both purposes.) In 1975, the constitutional oath was administered in the conference room with only justices present, and shortly thereafter the statutory oath was administered in the courtroom. Except for Byron White (whom I met at Pearl Harbor during World War II), my oldest and closest friend present at the first oath-taking was Tom Clark.

The chief justice also oversees relationships between the federal courts and their sister institutions. He is, after all, not just the top federal judicial officer and the leader of the United States Supreme Court but also the chief justice of the United States. And, as time permits, he serves as principal host to the many foreign dignitaries who visit the Court.

Other special responsibilities of the chief often surprise people. By an act of Congress, the chief justice is a member of the board of regents of the Smithsonian Institution, and by a tradition dating back to Roger Taney, the chief justice serves as chancellor and presides over that board, which includes the vice president, six members of Congress, and nine distinguished private citizens.

Finally, the chief is, in effect, the CEO of the Supreme Court Building. Like any good executive, he has many able assistants, including the highly qualified counselor to the chief justice, the clerk of the court, the marshal, the librarian, and the reporter of decisions. Together, this team oversees the several hundred men and women who every day maintain the beautiful and historic Supreme Court Building, open it to crowds of tourists, and ensure that it serves lawyers and litigants.

To sustain the high morale of the workforce at the Court, the chief presides at an annual awards ceremony before the end of each term. Cash awards are given to employees who have made exceptional contributions to the operation of the Court during the preceding year, and length-of-service medals are presented to employees who have multiples of five years of government service. Members of the exceptional Supreme Court police force are always well represented among the recipients of both kinds of awards. One of the traditions that has impressed me ever since my arrival as a law clerk in 1947 is the ability of every Supreme Court police officer to recognize a new employee within hours after he or she first reports for work; no identification badge is required to ensure a friendly greeting. Moreover, their ability to maintain order in the courtroom is demonstrated by the fact that disrespectful conduct almost never occurs; in the only instance that I can remember, the discourteous visitor was so promptly and silently removed that the proceeding continued without interruption.

III

Fred Vinson

Fred M. Vinson, Chief Justice (1946–1953)

F RED VINSON WAS BORN in 1890 in northeastern Kentucky; he graduated at the top of his class from Centre College, in the city of Danville. After returning to Lawrence County, he embarked on a career of public service. He became a city attorney, then served in the Army during World War I. In 1924, he was elected to Congress, where he remained for fourteen years. While there, he met and befriended Senator Harry Truman, ultimately becoming a confidant of and a participant in card games with the future president. President Roosevelt nominated him as a judge on the United States Court of Appeals for the District of Columbia Circuit in 1937. One of his colleagues on that court was Wiley B. Rutledge, who would later become a justice of the Supreme Court and my first boss after I finished law school.

In 1943 Vinson resigned from the court of appeals to become the second director of the Office of Economic Stabilization — the agency that oversaw the rationing of items in short supply and imposed price and wage regulations on the wartime economy. (The first director of that agency was James F. Byrnes, who had been appointed to the Supreme Court a few months before the outbreak of World War II and had resigned from the Court on October 3, 1942, to accept the newly created position.) Vinson ran that agency during the war, and then President Truman selected him as his secretary of the treasury. In 1946, after Chief Justice Stone suffered his fatal cerebral hemorrhage, Truman nominated and the Senate by voice vote confirmed Vinson to be chief justice of the United States. He served until his death, on September 8, 1953, a few months before *Brown* v. *Board of Education* was to be reargued.

Willard Pedrick, a young lawyer who had worked for Vinson as a law clerk on the court of appeals and in an executive capacity during the war, joined the faculty of Northwestern University Law School shortly after I became a student, in the fall of 1945. He was the source of the cordial relationship between Chief Justice Vinson and Northwestern that developed later.

My relationship to Vinson had its roots in the spring of 1947, when I was finishing law school and Congress statutorily increased the funds available for the employment of law clerks. The increase enabled four associate justices — including Justice Rutledge — to hire two law clerks each year, while the chief justice hired three. The chief received the extra law clerk because his chambers reviewed all of the *in forma pauperis* petitions (cases in which the petitioner is too poor to incur the cost of printing relevant court documents) that indigent prisoners filed to challenge the constitutionality of their convictions. It was the job of the chief's clerks to prepare memoranda summarizing each such petition and recommending an appropriate disposition. Each of the associate justices received a carbon copy of the original typed document; almost invariably, the chief's clerk recommended "deny," explaining that the prisoner had not exhausted his state remedies or that the claim had no merit.

Before Vinson began employing a third clerk, the substantial burden that *in forma pauperis* petitions imposed might also have been alleviated by relieving the chief's chambers of the responsibility to make a preliminary review of each *in forma pauperis* petition. When the same problem arose some years later — after the number of *in forma pauperis* petitions increased dramatically from 1946 levels — the latter course was followed, and the clerk's office began making copies of all *in forma pauperis* filings and distributing them to all nine chambers for individual review. Given the state of copying technology in 1946, however, Congress apparently decided that an extra law clerk's salary of $5,400 was a bargain in comparison to the cost of making nine copies of each one of those papers.

When that statute was passed, Art Seder and I were coeditors of the law review at Northwestern with grade point averages that placed us at the top of the graduating class. We were then completing a three-year course of study in an accelerated program that consumed just two calendar years. The program was popular because most members of the class were recently discharged veterans of World War II eager to become productive participants in the civilian economy as soon as possible. Art, for example, had flown twenty-five missions over Germany as the pilot of a four-engine B-17 bomber, and I had spent most of the war at Pearl Harbor studying intercepted Japanese radio transmissions. I think there were only three women in the entire law school at that time.

That spring, two of our professors — Willard Pedrick, whom I have already described, and Willard Wirtz, who had been on the faculty at the University of Iowa's law school when Wiley Rutledge was the dean and who later became the secretary of labor

Wiley B. Rutledge, Associate Justice (1943–1949). 1947, oil on canvas by Harold Brett. *Collection of the Supreme Court of the United States.*

in John F. Kennedy's and Lyndon Johnson's administrations — advised us that they had persuaded two Supreme Court justices to hire Northwestern graduates as law clerks. One prospect was for a one-year job beginning at the end of the summer with Justice Wiley Rutledge, and the other was for a two-year job with Chief Justice Vinson beginning a year later. They told us that they considered us equally qualified and that they could not decide which of us to support for which clerkship. They delegated the decision to us. I won the coin flip and reported for duty with Justice Rutledge in September. Art began his work with the chief justice a year later. The other seven justices active during our tenures as clerks were Hugo Black, Stanley Reed, Felix Frankfurter, William Douglas, Frank Murphy, Robert Jackson, and Harold Burton.

My appraisal of Chief Justice Vinson is based on my own clerkship, what I learned later from Art, and, of course, information in the public domain. Fred Vinson was President Truman's second appointee to the Court. Truman had previously appointed Harold Burton, who had served with him in the Senate, and he later appointed Sherman Minton, also a former colleague in the Senate, and Tom Clark, who was his attorney general when Art and I were in law school. Burton was the only Republican that Truman named. Because each of Truman's nominees had previously worked closely with him in the Senate or the executive branch, it is fair to infer that the president's firsthand knowledge about their characters and qualifications played a more important role in his selection than any recommendations made by lawyers, bar associations, or political sponsors.

In 1948, during the spring of my clerkship, President Truman hosted a reception at the White House for federal judges and their clerks. As a Republican, I was not a special admirer of Truman, but I still vividly remember the favorable impression that he made when he greeted me in the receiving line. He was a genuine, friendly guy whom I liked right away. So, although I voted for Dewey in the election that fall, I found myself pulling for Truman while listening to the returns.

I did so despite my adverse reaction to the timing of his appointment of Rutledge's successor a few weeks earlier. A year after my clerkship with him ended, Justice Rutledge had a stroke while driving, and he died two weeks later, on September 10, 1949, at the age of fifty-five. Because his excellence as a scholar and a judge was so well established, his premature death was an especially sad occasion for his host of friends and admirers. As I left the church following the funeral services, I was startled to find a newsboy hawking papers with headlines proclaiming that Truman had nominated Sherman Minton to fill Rutledge's seat. Perhaps my grief at the time has colored my views, but I thought then and have often commented since that Truman's announcement was an unnecessarily prompt and somewhat disrespectful response to a tragic event.

I recall mentioning this to Tom Clark in the 1970s. After serving as attorney general, Clark was appointed to the Supreme Court by Truman, and he proved to be unquestionably the strongest of the four Supreme Court appointments that Truman made. As I explained, we became good friends while I served on the Seventh Circuit Court of Appeals. His response to my comment sheds some light on the process by which Truman nominated Supreme Court justices.

Sherman Minton was a judge on the Seventh Circuit Court of Appeals; he had formerly served with Truman in the Senate. Tom told me that Minton was at home in New Albany, Indiana, when he read the newspaper's report of Rutledge's death. He immediately bought a railroad ticket, boarded the overnight train to Washington, and, upon his arrival, took a taxi to the

White House. Without any advance notice, he arrived at the gate, identified himself, and told the guard that he wanted to see the president. He was promptly admitted and taken to the Oval Office. As Tom Clark related, Minton simply told his friend, former colleague, and the current president that he wanted the job that Rutledge's death had made available. Truman agreed on the spot, and Minton became his third appointment to the Court soon thereafter. Perhaps I am prejudiced, but I never thought that he had a love or understanding of the law remotely comparable to Rutledge's.

I know nothing about the process that Truman followed when he selected Fred Vinson to succeed Harlan Stone. In light of Clark's story, however, it is reasonable to infer that a friendship that included regular poker games and frequent telephone conversations played a role in the decision.

In his first term as chief justice, Vinson selected Byron White as one of his law clerks. Byron was an All-American athlete in football and basketball, a Rhodes Scholar, a World War II Navy intelligence officer who had survived kamikaze attacks in the Pacific, and a top graduate of Yale's law school. He was also the first former law clerk to become a justice. (Bill Rehnquist was the second, I was the third, and Stephen Breyer — who clerked for Justice Arthur Goldberg — was the fourth.) Byron was appointed to the Court by President Kennedy in 1962 and served for thirty-one years. It was Byron's conduct as a clerk that gave rise to the Court's adoption of a strict rule that has remained in place for sixty-five years. Byron regularly shot baskets in the gym on the third floor, which was immediately above the courtroom. On one occasion, he was practicing layups as his boss was presiding over an oral argument in the room below him. Whether the sound of his bouncing ball had an impact on the outcome of that case is not known, but Byron never denied responsibility for Vinson's promulgation of an unwritten rule that is still in effect today: While the law clerks are allowed regular late-afternoon games — in which, by the way, Byron participated for years after becoming a justice — no basketball is permitted in the gym while the Court is in session.

It is quite clear that President Truman continued to have the greatest respect for Vinson in the years after he became chief justice. For instance, in 1948, when relations with the Soviets were at a particularly low ebb, the president considered sending Vinson to Russia on a diplomatic mission. Vinson mentioned this proposed mission to Moscow to his law clerks so often that Art became excited about the possibility that Vinson might take a law clerk with him. Instead, the State Department torpedoed the idea.

This closeness did not, however, prevent deference in Vinson's interactions with Truman. Well aware of the men's warm relationship, Art Seder was surprised to overhear Vinson address his close friend as Mr. President in a telephone conversation.

That deference may have influenced Vinson's vote in the landmark case of *Youngstown Sheet & Tube Co.* v. *Sawyer* (1952). That case arose during the Korean War, when defense contractors needed massive amounts of steel. Concerned that an impending strike would disrupt the steel supply, Truman seized control of the mills. The steel companies sued, challenging the constitutionality of the seizure, and the Court held, by a vote of six to three, that the executive power vested in the president by Article II of the Constitution did not authorize his seizure of privately owned steel mills, despite the existence of a national emergency. The fact that two Truman appointees — Justices Burton and Clark — joined the Court's judgment exemplifies the independence of the federal judiciary. Although the three dissenters included the two other Truman appointees — the chief justice and Justice Minton — the fact that Justice Reed joined the

Arthur Seder, law clerk to Chief Justice Vinson (1948–1949 term). *Used with permission of Arthur Seder.*

chief's dissent demonstrates that this position, too, was not without arguable merit. (There is a nonfrivolous rumor that the president's decision to seize the steel mills may have been influenced by something that Vinson said while playing poker with him one evening during the emergency.) The limits on the power of the president imposed by that decision have been respected ever since.

Art Seder regarded Vinson as a confident and competent chief. Though a decisive judge, he was by no means the intellectual leader of the Court. Three of his colleagues — Felix Frankfurter, Bill Douglas, and Wiley Rutledge — had exceptional and superior academic credentials. Frankfurter had been among the nation's leading public intellectuals while a professor at Harvard Law School before joining the Court. Though Douglas's academic tenure was shorter, it was also distinguished, and it included positions at Columbia and then Yale. Wiley Rutledge's law school teaching matured in deanships, first at the Washington University School of Law and then at the University of Iowa School of Law. Three members of the Court — Hugo Black, Robert Jackson, and Stanley Reed — had extensive experience in trial and appellate litigation, which Vinson did not. Black worked as a private attorney, prosecutor, and local judge before leading investigations as a United States senator for Alabama. Prior to Jackson's appointment to the Court, he had been both solicitor general and attorney general in FDR's administration. And Reed had also served as solicitor general before joining the bench. To quote Art: "One would think Vinson might have been a little overwhelmed — he a country lawyer from a small town in Kentucky — sitting at the head of a table surrounded by law professors and others whose careers had been made in the practice of law. But if so, he never gave any open sign of discomfort."

Vinson was not a writer either and may have had a little difficulty following some of the more esoteric arguments advanced by counsel. Nonetheless, he had confidence in his ability to identify which outcome of a case would, in his judgment, best serve the public interest. In Art's words, he "gave his law clerks very few instructions about *how* they should write drafts of his opinions, but he was very clear about the result he wanted." In discussing cases with his clerks after the Saturday conferences, Vinson cogently described the positions of each justice and readily answered the clerks' questions. Those candid and detailed post-conference sessions made it clear to his clerks that the chief was well qualified to serve as the equal of every one of his colleagues.

Sharing the views of other law clerks during the 1947 term (and thus not including Art Seder's), I was not an especial admirer of the chief. My boss was frequently one of four dissenters. In Fourth Amendment cases, he and Frank Murphy shared the views of Frankfurter and Jackson, while in antitrust cases they tended to agree with Black and Douglas. I do not recall any five-to-four decisions in which Vinson and Rutledge agreed, but I do recall one case in which it was Rutledge who wrote for the majority over Vinson's dissent. Only one other justice — Jackson — dissented from my boss's narrowly written opinion in that case, *Bob-Lo Excursion Co.* v. *Michigan* (1948).

Bob-Lo presented the Court with an opportunity to overrule its unfortunate precedent in *Hall* v. *DeCuir* (1878). In *DeCuir,* the Louisiana Supreme Court had affirmed an award of damages to a woman of color who had boarded a steamboat in New Orleans, Louisiana, to travel to Hermitage, Louisiana, and then been refused accommodation in a cabin set apart for white persons. The Supreme Court reversed on the ground that because Louisiana's attempt to protect its citizens from racial discrimination involved an interstate carrier — the steamship continued on to Mississippi, where state law could require separate accommodation for nonwhite passengers — its actions violated the commerce clause of the federal Constitution. Today that Court decision seems patently wrong because the Louisiana court was simply enforcing a state law that was fully consistent with the objectives of the then recently enacted post–Civil War amendments as well as the common-law duties of public carriers. It is also remarkable because the Court thought that its result was compelled by the absence of congressional action — that is, it thought that the Constitution barred Louisiana's ban on race discrimination when Congress had said no such thing.

In *Bob-Lo,* the owner of a vessel that made daily round trips between Detroit and a Canadian island in the lower Detroit River argued that the enforcement of its "whites only" policy against an African American high school student enjoyed similar constitutional immunity, in this case from a Michigan antidiscrimination statute, because its vessel was engaged in foreign commerce. In an uncharacteristically short majority opinion, Justice Rutledge distinguished the *DeCuir* case — which is to say, explained that it was relevantly different from *Bob-Lo* — on the narrow ground that unlike the potential conflict between the Mississippi and Louisiana laws, in *Bob-Lo*, Michigan law, Canadian law, and federal law all prohibited discrimination on the basis of race and so presented no risk to carriers of conflicting legal obligations. Justice Douglas, joined by Justice Black, indicated in a concurring opinion that they would have overruled *DeCuir*. The chief, by contrast, joined Justice Jackson's dissenting view that the interest in protecting foreign

Formal group photograph of the 1946 Vinson Court.

Seated from left: Justices Felix Frankfurter, Hugo L. Black, Chief Justice Fred M. Vinson, and Justices Stanley Reed and William O. Douglas. Standing from left: Justices Wiley Rutledge, Frank Murphy, Robert H. Jackson, and Harold H. Burton. C. 1946. *By Harris & Ewing, Collection of the Supreme Court of the United States.*

commerce from burdensome state laws was of primary importance. The dissenters' reliance on *DeCuir* suggests that they were less concerned about discrimination against a nonwhite passenger than about the modest — indeed, trivial — potential burden on the shipowner. In the end, the Court affirmed the judgment finding the defendant guilty of violating Michigan's Civil Rights Act and requiring the company to pay a fine of twenty-five dollars.

The cases in which Rutledge dissented that troubled me the most were *Bute* v. *Illinois* (1948), holding that Illinois did not have to appoint counsel for a defendant charged with a felony carrying a twenty-year sentence, and *Ahrens* v. *Clark* (1948), holding that enemy aliens did not have access to the writ of habeas corpus because they were being detained on Ellis Island rather than in the District of Columbia, where their custodian — the attorney general — was located. Happily, both of those cases have since been overruled. Indeed, in a recent narcotic-possession case, the Court held that even an alien's right to counsel may be violated by a lawyer's incorrect advice that his guilty plea would not lead to his deportation. And rejection of the narrow reading of the habeas corpus statute played a critical role in the Court's conclusion that the writ was available to detainees in Guantánamo. Even terrorists allegedly sharing responsibility for the attack on the World Trade Center on September 11, 2001, may seek judicial review of the basis for their detention.

Despite my misgivings about Vinson's judgment in some of the cases that the Court decided during my one-year clerkship, he undoubtedly came out on the right side in the two most important cases of the term, both of which he authored. Those opinions came in the restrictive-covenant cases *Shelley* v. *Kraemer* (1948) and *Hurd* v. *Hodge* (1948), which provided me with an opportunity to see Thurgood Marshall — then chief counsel for the NAACP — argue before the Court (he also argued three other cases that term). Justice Rutledge and two other justices did not participate in those cases, presumably because they owned property burdened with covenants prohibiting their sale to African Americans. If there had been a three-to-three vote among the six justices who were not disqualified, they would merely have entered an order stating that the judgments had been affirmed by an equally divided Court. Fortunately, however, they unanimously held that judicial action enforcing such covenants is prohibited by the Constitution. Their exceptional importance merits brief comment.

The first of the two restrictive-covenant cases arose in Missouri and Michigan. The decision rested on an interpretation of the equal protection clause of the Fourteenth Amendment — a provision that prohibits "any State" from denying to any person within its jurisdiction "the equal protection of the laws." The decision prohibited a widespread and odious form of racial discrimination in every state of the union. Because the second case arose in the District of Columbia — which, of course, is not a state — the Fourteenth Amendment was inapplicable. In order to reach the same result in that case, it was necessary for the Court to find another source for the government's duty to govern impartially that was expressly protected by the Fourteenth Amendment. Vinson found two: a federal statute applicable to Washington, D.C., that stated the same policy as the Fourteenth Amendment and a rule announced in earlier cases that federal courts should not enforce private agreements that contravened the public policy of the United States, including the requirement of equal protection expressed in the Fourteenth Amendment. Thus, simple justice rather than constitutional text dictated the result. Together, the two cases protected the right of an African American to purchase property anywhere in the United States despite the existence of a covenant prohibiting the purchase from taking place.

Because of the importance of these holdings, the chief justice appropriately assigned himself the opinions in both cases. I have always believed that they were drafted by his clerk Frank Allen, a brilliant scholar who later became dean of the University of Michigan Law School. Frank was also a graduate of Northwestern; the quality of his work, like that of Art's, no doubt influenced Vinson's later decisions to have two Northwestern graduates as law clerks during succeeding terms.

While the chief justice is an equal of the other justices when he votes on a case, he is first among them in shaping many of the internal workings of the Court. It is here that some chiefs have had their greatest influence. Indeed, the procedures that Chief Justice Fred Vinson followed are quite different from those in place today.

While the Court has continued the Vinson-era practice of holding seven two-week oral argument sessions during each term, the number of argument days in each of those weeks has been reduced; whereas there were five a week under Vinson, there are only three a week today. Except for the few cases on what was called, in the Vinson period, the summary docket, each side was allowed a full hour for argument.

What is now a two-hour morning session beginning at 10:00 was, when Vinson was chief, a session that began at noon and lasted until 2:00 p.m. There was then a half-hour luncheon break before the Court reconvened at 2:30, meaning that hungry justices sometimes ate a little too much and found it difficult to remain alert during the afternoon session, which lasted until 4:30. On more than one occasion, Justice Rutledge thought it necessary to give Frank Murphy, his neighbor on the bench, a jab or two to make sure that he was awake.

The questioning of advocates at oral argument during Vinson's tenure reflected the particular personalities of contemporary members of the Court. On occasion, Justice Rutledge returned to chambers after argument quite obviously pleased with the fact that an experienced lawyer had been unable to make an effective response to his question. I have no memory of any questioning by the chief. I do recall, however, that the justice who was by far the most active in posing questions to counsel during oral arguments was Felix Frankfurter. Sometimes I received the impression that he had not yet read the briefs and was relying on counsel to identify the exact issue in dispute. On other occasions he treated the advocate in a way that reminded me of a law professor dealing with a student who needed to be told what earlier cases had decided. I recall one colloquy with Thurgood Marshall, then an attorney appearing before the Court, in which Felix reiterated his understanding of a precedent several times and Thurgood firmly adhered to his position, respectfully stating more than once: "That is not how I read the case." Though Thurgood was unlikely to win that point with Felix, he was a remarkably talented advocate. For example, in arguing a challenge to segregated legal education in *Sipuel* v. *Board of Regents of the University of Oklahoma,* Thurgood was so persuasive that his oral arguments ended on a Thursday and on the following Monday the Court ordered the University of Oklahoma to admit his client, Ada Sipuel, to its law school. Years later, while playing golf with an Oklahoma graduate who had been one of Ada Sipuel's classmates, I was pleased to learn that the students had welcomed her as a friend despite the state's attempt to enforce its exclusionary policy.

The five-days-a-week oral argument schedule under Vinson made it necessary for the Court to set Saturdays aside for the conferences at which the justices discussed and usually decided the merits of each case. Those conferences differed from those held in recent years in three significant ways — the processing of petitions for review, the determination of what opinions were ready for public announcement, and the discussion of how to decide the cases argued during the preceding week.

The normal procedure in the Saturday conferences in 1947 included a discussion of almost every petition requesting that the Court review a lower court decision; the only exceptions were a relatively small number of cases that the chief considered too frivolous to merit discussion. He would identify those cases on a dead list circulated on Friday, but even cases that the chief had dead-listed would be discussed if any member of the Court so requested.

During the time that Vinson was the chief, however, that strong presumption in favor of discussing almost every case ready for disposition changed. Since 1950, the reverse presumption has maintained. Under the new procedure, before each conference, the chief justice circulates a discuss list, identifying cases ready for disposition that he considers worthy of discussion. Any justice may add cases to that list, but other than those additions, the requests for review that failed to make the discuss list will be denied. This difference in procedure is adequately justified by the fact that only 1,510 cases were filed in Chief Justice Vinson's first term in 1946 whereas 8,521 filings occurred during Chief Justice Roberts's first term in 2005.

In the Vinson era, when the print shop returned the first printed draft of an opinion to its author, his messenger delivered one copy of it to each of the eight other justices' chambers. In the Rutledge chambers — and I assume in the others as well — that copy went directly to the justice, who normally responded without even consulting his law clerk unless the draft presented a question prompting further deliberation. If the responding justice agreed with the draft, he would usually write the words *Please join me* on the draft itself and return it to the author. The Saturday conference would be the occasion when the author could inform his colleagues about the status of his circulating opinions.

Today, first drafts are circulated in multiple copies, enabling law clerks to provide the justice with comments before the justice joins, suggests changes, or advises the author that he or she intends to write separately. During my years on the Court, I used the traditional "please join me" formula for expressing my unqualified agreement with the author, even though my join was written in a separate letter rather than on the back of a copy of the opinion. And since copies of join letters, as well as letters asking for changes or announcing planned dissents, are now routinely circulated to all chambers, there is seldom any need for an extended discussion of the status of circulating opinions.

The most important business at conference is the decision of the cases that have been argued and submitted since the prior conference. In the 1947 term, the chief justice introduced the discussion of each case, and the other justices then spoke in order of seniority. (Because there was no limit on the time that each might speak, I understand that Justice Frankfurter occasionally provided his colleagues with comments akin to a fifty-minute classroom lecture.) After everyone had had an opportunity to speak, the voting began. The junior justice voted first, followed by the others, in reverse order of seniority.

Sometime between 1947 and 1975, when I joined the Court, it became regular practice for the justices to announce their votes during their initial comments. Bill Rehnquist, before he became the chief, and I sometimes stated that we thought that the practice followed during the years when we had been law clerks was preferable because, as the two most junior justices, we thought our opportunity to persuade our more senior colleagues was lessened once they had announced their votes. When he served as the chief, however, Bill's views on this issue changed. Mine have not.

The staff of the entire Court, as well as the staff in each justice's chambers, is larger today than it was in 1947. Instead of one or two law clerks, each associate justice is now authorized to employ four. Notwithstanding this increase in the clerk-to-justice ratio, there is now more interaction between justices and clerks working in other chambers than there was in 1947. The justices now have a joint reception to which all clerks are invited; the clerks in each chamber customarily invite each of the other justices to lunch once a term; and there is both a Christmas party and an end-of-term party to which all justices and clerks are invited. No such routine contact between justices and clerks working in other chambers occurred in 1947. Like all of the other clerks, I did, however, have a number of spontaneous and stimulating conversations with Justice Frankfurter. (A topic to which he returned more than once with me and others was what he regarded as the Court's mistaken conclusion that tidelands oil belonged to the federal government rather than to the coastal states.) I think all of us had some occasional contact with every other member of the Court. I especially recall one meeting with Justice Black, and another with the chief.

Justice Black, a former United States senator who had excelled in the competitive world of electoral politics before joining the Court, played tennis regularly on a court in the backyard of his home in Alexandria. He once invited me to play singles with him. During the ride to his house, he impressed me as a gentle, soft-spoken man; on the court he turned into a fierce competitor. I easily won the first set, but he was the victor in a long, hard-fought second set. I was really disheartened and surprised that a sixty-two-year-old man was in so much better physical condition than I was.

As chief justice, Fred Vinson was ably assisted by Edith McHugh, an especially competent secretary who might also have been characterized as somewhat officious. Art Seder told me that she kept track of the number of times that the chief disagreed with his clerks' recommendations on whether to grant or deny petitions for certiorari, and she seemed to enjoy giving the clerks what she regarded as failing grades. My foremost memory of her concerns a morning that she called Justice Rutledge's secretary, Edna Lindgreen. Edith advised Edna that the chief justice wanted to meet with Justice Rutledge, quite obviously expecting that Justice Rutledge would come to the chief's chambers to do so. When Edna conveyed this apparent summons to Justice Rutledge, he told her to advise the chief's secretary that he would be happy to welcome the chief whenever it was convenient for the chief to come to our chambers. My memory of Vinson's arrival a few minutes later is a continuing reminder of the status of the chief justice as just one of nine equally powerful decision-makers.

In 1947, commuting to and from work was one area in which there was not complete equality among all nine members of the Court. Each justice had a messenger responsible for delivering papers to the chambers of other justices and for serving lunch to his boss. The justices ate (and paid for) the food that was prepared in the public cafeteria, sometimes eating in the justices' spacious dining room on the second floor and sometimes in their own chambers. The messenger was available to drive for the justice (or his wife) in the justice's own car. Chief Justice Vinson's car and driver were, on occasion, put at Mrs. Vinson's service. When that happened, Vinson's law clerk might be given a particular non-legal assignment. As Art Seder described it, "When Mrs. Vinson had commandeered the chief's car and it was time to go home, he frequently asked me for a ride in my car. I had a beat-up old 1938 Ford at the time, but the chief squeezed himself in and we rattled and bumped our way to the Wardman Park, where they lived. There the doorman was always ready to order me off the premises

until he saw the chief justice emerging from the car, when his atti-
tude changed markedly. I always enjoyed that experience."

Chief Justice Vinson also contributed to one of my earliest and
more memorable professional successes in private practice. While
still a law clerk in 1947, I helped Justice Rutledge draft his concurring opinion in *Marino* v. *Ragen,* a case reviewing a denial by
the circuit court of Winnebago County, Illinois, of Marino's
application for a writ of habeas corpus challenging the constitutionality of his conviction. Illinois law did not provide for appellate review of such orders in the state system. As a result, the only
Court with jurisdiction to review the state trial judge's denial of
the writ was the Supreme Court of the United States.

Marino had been in prison since 1925 as a result of having
pleaded guilty to murder. He had been eighteen years old at the
time, in the country for less than two years, and unable to speak
English. No lawyer was appointed to represent him; instead, the
arresting officer served as his interpreter. After the case arrived in
our Court, the Illinois attorney general confessed error, acknowledging both that Marino's twenty-two-year-old conviction was
invalid and that Marino had invoked the proper state remedy.
Justice Rutledge joined the judgment setting aside Marino's conviction but wrote separately to explain why he believed that the
three postconviction remedies available to Illinois prisoners —
common-law writ of error, habeas corpus, and *coram nobis* —
constituted a procedural labyrinth made up entirely of blind
alleys. In his judgment, these arcane procedures were virtually
useless, and the possibility that the Illinois attorney general
might eventually confess error in flagrant cases was not an

adequate state remedy. He noted that during the preceding three terms, about half of all the *in forma pauperis* petitions alleging violations of constitutional rights had been filed by Illinois prisoners.

Just over a year later, possibly influenced by Rutledge's opinion, the Illinois General Assembly enacted a new postconviction remedies act that simplified the procedures available to convicted prisoners. In a speech to the American Law Institute in 1949, Vinson commented favorably on the state's elimination of its "blind alleys," noting that many, if not most, of the cases in which the Court has spelled out the requirements of a fair trial had come up as *in forma pauperis* petitions.

Despite the clarity of the text of the new Illinois statute, state judges continued to use boilerplate orders to deny prisoners any hearing in cases asserting constitutional claims. Finally, in 1951, in three cases argued by my former law professor and ongoing role model Nat Nathanson and decided in an opinion written by Chief Justice Vinson, the Court effectively directed the Illinois Supreme Court to decide whether the state statute meant what it seemed to.

When the case was sent back to Illinois for further proceedings in state court, I was practicing law, and Nat asked me to represent two of the three petitioners, Julius Bernard Sherman and Arthur La Frana. I agreed to do so. On my first trip to the state prison in Joliet, I interviewed Sherman, who alleged that the police had forced him to sign his confession. In the text of the confession, he had written something to this effect: "I have signed this confession because I insisted on doing so." It seemed likely that that comment had been dictated by a threatening police officer rather than composed by Sherman himself, so I expected to meet a client eager to tell his side of the story in open court. Instead, I met a man who could have been a defensive tackle for the Chicago Bears and who showed little interest in discussing his pending case. It was not that he was not happy to see me; he was. But he welcomed me as a lawyer for another reason. As he explained, he needed advice about how to patent the invention that he was perfecting. When I asked him to describe his invention, he identified it as a new method of digging tunnels. While I respected his judgment about the possible utility and demand for such a device in Joliet, I was unable to assist him.

My visit to Joliet to interview Arthur La Frana was more productive. He had been convicted of murdering a theater cashier in 1937. His petition under the new postconviction remedies act alleged that the police had handcuffed his arms behind his back, hoisted him until his feet almost left the floor, and then beat him until he agreed to confess. Unlike Sherman, La Frana did not have a particularly striking physical appearance. He was of average size and did not look like a man who would assault a defenseless victim. He was courteous and articulate. The most memorable moment of our first meeting came when I asked him to describe the most severe pain caused by the handcuffs, expecting him first to refer to his wrists. He instead described excruciating pain in his upper arms and shoulders. I was surprised but also convinced that he was telling the truth. That conviction motivated a more thorough search for corroborating evidence than I might otherwise have undertaken. Among the evidence that we found was a county jail medical record describing the injuries to his wrists, a news photo taken of La Frana when the police announced that they had solved the case, the testimony of his former wife, who was present in the police station at the time, and the information that several days elapsed between the confession and his transfer from police custody to the county jail. Most persuasive, however, was the incredible explanation for his injuries offered by the police captain: La Frana had fallen down the stairs when allowed to use the men's room. There was simply no possibility that the fall the captain described could have produced the injuries that the record established. There was also no explanation for the delay in transferring custody of La Frana to the county jail other than officers' hope that the healing process would eliminate the bruises that appeared in the photograph that we made a part of the record.

Ultimately, the Illinois Supreme Court ruled in our favor, and La Frana was released. A critical step in the process that led to the termination of his seventeen years of wrongful incarceration was the opinion that Fred Vinson announced in 1951.

IV

Earl Warren

Earl Warren, Chief Justice (1953–1969)

CHIEF JUSTICE FRED VINSON'S death in office on September 8, 1953, gave President Eisenhower his first opportunity to fill a vacancy on the Court. It took him less than three weeks to make his decision. On September 27, 1953, Attorney General Herbert Brownell flew to California to convey the president's choice in person to the man selected: Governor Earl Warren. Warren immediately agreed to accept the appointment.

In naming Warren, Eisenhower nominated one of the most popular politicians of the day. Warren's career had been a series of successes: prosecuting attorney for Alameda County, attorney general of California, and then governor of that state. In 1942 he was elected governor on the Republican ticket, and in 1946 his reelection was unopposed because he received the nomination of not only his own party but the Democratic and Progressive Parties as well. In 1948 he was the vice presidential candidate on New York governor Thomas Dewey's Republican presidential ticket, which was narrowly and surprisingly defeated by Harry Truman. Warren's importance continued to grow after he joined the Court.

As chief justice, Warren has been described as the "Super Chief" who drove an "engine of reform" from 1953 to 1969. But there is a question of the exact date he became the engineer. Three days after Warren accepted Eisenhower's nomination, Eisenhower announced at a press conference that he was making a "recess appointment" of Earl Warren as chief justice of the United

States. Later that day, Warren sent a telegram accepting the nomination and also made a more formal statement to the same effect. The written evidence of the appointment was dated October 2, 1953, and he took the oath of office three days later, on the first Monday in October.

At that time, the Court heard no oral arguments during the first week of the term. Instead, it held conferences to dispose of the certiorari petitions and jurisdictional statements that had been filed during the summer recess. Because he was unfamiliar with the procedures followed during conferences among the justices, Warren asked Hugo Black, the most senior associate justice, to preside.

During that initial period, and indeed until March of the following year, it is arguable that Earl Warren was not entitled to act as the first among equals. Article II of the Constitution provides that the "President shall have Power to fill up all Vacancies that may happen during the Recess of the Senate, by granting Commissions which shall expire at the End of their next Session." President Eisenhower and Attorney General Brownell relied on that provision as the basis for filling the vacancy caused by the death of Fred Vinson during a recess of the Senate. Earl Warren and his future colleagues acquiesced in that literal reading of the words "all Vacancies."

There is tension, however, between that reading of Article II and the provision in Article III that states that the "Judges, both of the supreme and inferior Courts, shall hold their Offices during good Behaviour." A recess appointment must expire at the end of the "next Session" of the Senate; a judge's good behavior, one hopes, will persist somewhat longer. To prevent premature expiration of Earl Warren's tenure as chief justice, President Eisenhower took additional action that unquestionably authorized Warren to serve as the chief as long as he behaved himself. On January 12, 1954, the president sent his nomination to the Senate. The Judiciary Committee then held three days of hearings and, by a vote of twelve to three, recommended confirmation by the full Senate. On March 1, the nomination was confirmed by a voice vote; the president signed Warren's commission the next day, and on March 20, 1954, Warren was sworn in for the second time.

The dissenting votes of three senators on the Judiciary Committee illustrate how a hostile Senate could have used its power to decline to confirm a nominee and thus bring Earl Warren's tenure as chief justice to an end, notwithstanding his continuing "good Behaviour." Moreover, reflection on the underlying reasons for providing federal judges with life tenure — to ensure their impartiality and independence — has persuaded me that the president's power to make recess appointments does not include the power to make judicial appointments. It surely does not apply to vacancies in the legislative branch, for the Constitution commits the power to fill vacant congressional seats to state voters and officials. In my judgment, the president's power to make recess appointments should be construed as limited to vacancies in the executive branch of the government. I therefore treat March 20, 1954, rather than the date of his recess appointment, a little more than six months earlier, as the date when Earl Warren became the chief justice. Perhaps that date is merely a matter of academic interest because Warren's contributions to the law occurred after his legitimate tenure began, but in my judgment future recess appointments of judges should be avoided.

In 1954, I was one of the three lawyers who had recently formed the firm of Rothschild, Stevens, and Barry. During Earl Warren's entire tenure as chief justice, I continued to practice in Chicago with Ed Rothschild and Jack Barry as my partners. I was thus primarily an observer, rather than a participant, in the work of the Court during those years.

Like the coin flip that decided whether Art Seder or I would clerk for Wiley Rutledge, an event over which my colleagues and I had no control led to a decision — this time to form a partnership — that had an enormous impact on my career. When Ed, Jack, and I passed the Illinois bar exam and were hired as associates in the firm of Poppenhusen, Johnston, Thompson, Raymond, and Mayer, the firm had a roster of twenty-eight lawyers, including both partners and associates. It was what was then considered a large firm. My boss was Edward R. Johnston, regarded by many as the leading antitrust lawyer in the country. The partner listed immediately before Johnston on the letterhead, Conrad Poppenhusen, was the firm's senior member, but he no longer came to work on a regular basis. The name that directly followed Johnston's was that of Floyd Thompson, who was also called "the Chief" because he had joined the Illinois Supreme Court at the age of thirty-two and then become its chief justice. Thompson was both a tough, widely respected trial lawyer and the tight-fisted managing partner of the firm.

Ed, Jack, and I met when the Chief decided that we would share Mr. Poppenhusen's office and secretary. A few weeks later we traveled to Springfield, the state capital, to be admitted to the bar. Rather than rewarding us for becoming lawyers, the Chief docked our pay for being out of the office on a working day. That decision was almost certainly the proximate cause of our commitment to one another to form our own firm as soon as it became feasible to do so.

The term *diversity* fairly describes the membership and clients of our partnership. Ed Rothschild had played varsity basketball at Harvard College, engaged in combat in France as an Army officer during World War II, and then performed outstandingly as a student at Harvard Law School. Jack was a first-string end on an undefeated Notre Dame football team coached by Frank Leahy, skippered a small ship that landed troops and evacuated wounded soldiers during the Normandy invasion, and graduated at the top of his Notre Dame Law School class. I played tennis on the B team at the University of Chicago, served in the Navy at Pearl Harbor during the war, and graduated from Northwestern University Law School. Ed was a Jew who lived in a North Shore suburb; Jack was a Catholic from the West Side; and I was a South Side WASP. Ed backed Adlai Stevenson as an Independent; Jack served as a Democratic precinct captain and had supported Dick Daley in his campaign to become clerk of Cook County; I was a Republican without any political experience or expertise.

The depth of the friendship and the mutual admiration that began in Mr. Poppenhusen's office never abated. Until it was necessary to define our respective interests in unpaid fees for past services when I left the practice to go on the bench in 1970, we never needed and never had a written partnership agreement.

Edward I. Rothschild, John Paul Stevens, and Norman J. Barry, partners in the Chicago law firm of Rothschild, Stevens, and Barry.

Having had two of the best lawyers in Chicago as partners back when I was confronting the wide variety of problems that arise on short notice in a busy private practice did far more to enhance my ability to resolve contested issues on the bench than did the excellent education that I received in law school.

The word *diversity* also describes our clients. We represented defendants as well as plaintiffs in commercial litigation and personal injury cases. My clients included large enterprises such as Foster Wheeler Corporation and the Cuneo Press, both of which did business on a nationwide basis; companies such as the publisher of the *Wichita Eagle* and the Bowman Dairy, which were leaders in local metropolitan areas; and individuals with a wide variety of personal problems.

By the luck of the draw, I also happened to represent a surprisingly large number of entrepreneurs who were distributors of products manufactured by others — coin-operated washing machines, auto parts, calculating equipment, magazines, automobiles, and soft drinks.

These distributors seemed to share certain qualities that set them apart from the senior executives of the major companies with which they did business. They were hard workers who devoted long hours to their businesses. A friendly outlook on life rather than punctilious adherence to rules of etiquette enabled them to get along well with their employees, their customers, and members of the general public. I don't remember any who had a college education, but they were uniformly intelligent — more so, in my judgment, than most executives in the corporate world who had earned graduate degrees in business administration.

Two incidents in London in or about 1957 — one involving a Chicago client of mine, the other involving Warren — suggest that the chief justice and my clients shared views about some social customs. This similarity is one reason that I have long believed that if Earl Warren had entered the private sector rather than the public, he would have owned his own successful business. The first incident involved my representation of Norm Niemi during an attempted negotiation of a renewal of his franchise to distribute calculating equipment manufactured in England and sold in America. Niemi was taller, stronger, better-looking, more alert, and funnier than either of the immaculately dressed British gentlemen with whom we negotiated. He also had a superior understanding of the relevant stateside market. The fact that he was wearing brown shoes made no impression on me until our hosts went out of their way to emphasize the importance of wearing black shoes on certain occasions. While that offensive digression must have been intended to give them some advantage in our negotiations, it merely generated hostility that led to an impasse and ultimately to litigation that was costly to the manufacturer and highly profitable to Norm.

Earl Warren, who was also a tall, handsome man, had a somewhat similar experience in England in 1957. While attending a meeting of the American Bar Association in London, he made a major speech to a large audience of British and American lawyers at which he was expected to appear in a morning coat and striped trousers. Not having been forewarned about this sartorial requirement, he wore a brown suit to address the assembly, which evidently offended his hosts. The reaction of the audience to his social gaffe apparently embarrassed Warren and led to his resignation from the ABA. Like Norm, the chief may have overreacted to trivial comments. I suspect, however, that both of them were offended by the implication that an American's informal brown apparel was an admission of inferiority.

That experience did not prevent Warren from playing a significant role in foreign affairs. He traveled widely when the Court was not in session, made numerous speeches to foreign groups — as many as eight in one day on a visit to Ireland — and attended and helped to organize international judicial conferences advocating world peace through law. His liberal opinions motivated "Impeach Earl Warren" campaigns by hostile stateside critics, but Solicitor General J. Lee Rankin's travels with Warren led him to remark that people living beyond the borders of the United States regarded Warren as "the greatest humanitarian in the Western Hemisphere since Abraham Lincoln." In 1963, President John Kennedy asked him to head the American delegation at the coronation of Pope Paul VI and made Air Force One available to enable him to attend a world peace conference during the same trip. President Johnson also provided him with the use of Air Force One for several goodwill missions abroad. His choice of Warren to head the commission to investigate the assassination of President Kennedy reflected Johnson's judgment that the chief was the most trustworthy man available in the entire country. When two of the top officials of the Justice Department, Nicholas Katzenbach and Archibald Cox, asked him to head the commission, Warren turned them down because he thought it had been a mistake for Justice Owen Roberts to lead the investigation of the Navy's failure to anticipate the Japanese attack on Pearl Harbor and for Justice Robert Jackson to take a leave of absence to serve as the lead prosecutor in the Nuremberg trials of German war criminals. Warren firmly believed that Supreme Court justices should not accept such nonjudicial assignments. Nevertheless, in a meeting at the White House, President Johnson persuaded Warren that he had a patriotic duty to take charge of the investigation. After accepting that responsibility, he took an active part in the commission's work. For example, he and Gerald Ford made a trip to Dallas, where they inspected the window on the sixth floor of the Texas School Book Depository where Lee Harvey Oswald fired the shots that killed the president and wounded John Connally, the governor of Texas. On that trip he and Ford also questioned Jack Ruby, who had killed Oswald, and authorized the use of polygraph tests to verify Ruby's explanation that his sole motive was to make it unnecessary for Jacqueline Kennedy to suffer the anguish of returning to Dallas to testify against Oswald. Warren's reluctance to accept an unwanted assignment did not impair the quality of his performance.

Both President Kennedy and President Johnson demonstrated their respect for Earl Warren by stopping in for a brief visit at an annual dinner hosted for the chief by his law clerks. (Kennedy was present in 1961 and Johnson in 1966.)

Those dinners were far from the only opportunities Warren's clerks had to socialize with the chief. Unlike his predecessor, Warren led a Court that heard no arguments on Fridays and that used that day to hold what would otherwise have been a weekly Saturday conference. The chief frequently took advantage of this flexibility in Saturday's schedule by inviting all of his clerks out for a social lunch. Warren's clerks also often spent time at his home watching sporting events. He apparently enjoyed conversations about politics more than judicial business during these outings, but their discussions about the Court did make it clear that Felix Frankfurter was not his favorite colleague, presumably because Frankfurter was so loquacious in explaining his own analyses of legal issues. On two occasions, after Felix announced a lengthy oral dissent in open court, Warren took it upon himself to provide the audience with an extemporaneous response to the dissent even though he was not the author of the majority opinion that Felix had criticized.

At the office, a formal set of rules governed clerks' access to their boss. Warren did not have an open-door policy for them because his "formidable secretary" guarded his door. That watchdog was Edith McHugh, the former secretary for Chief Justice Vinson, whom I have already mentioned. For her, the job of a clerk was by no means equal to hers, and other justices were not equal to her boss.

My most vivid memory of Chief Justice Earl Warren is from my one and only oral argument before the Supreme Court, in 1962. The image of Warren that remains fresh in my mind is not one of his asking me a question I could not answer or his reacting favorably to a clever argument that I had advanced. It is instead the very first glimpse of him that greeted me as I rose to address the Court. Startlingly, Warren loomed over me, appearing to be only inches away.

Although I had witnessed dozens of arguments, I had not realized how close the justices are to the lawyer who is addressing them. Many Supreme Court advocates who were far more experienced than I — including current justices John Roberts, Ruth Bader Ginsburg, and Elena Kagan — have told me that they retain a similar vivid recollection of their first oral arguments. Although the actual distance between the lectern and the bench is a little over six feet — and the distance between the advocate and the chief is about eleven feet — I was convinced that Chief Justice Warren could have shaken my hand had he wished.

In my argument on behalf of the Bowman Dairy Company I was defending the decision of a district court to dismiss a government antitrust case against Bowman and another dairy after some eleven years of litigation. In the trial court, the government had established against Bowman a prima facie violation of a federal antitrust law known as the Robinson-Patman Act. It had done so by proving that five specific independent stores paid higher prices than their chain-store competitors. To avoid liability, we had to show that this price difference was justified on permissible grounds, in this case because the costs of providing the independent stores with dairy products were higher than the costs of serving the chain stores. Among the costs on which we relied was time spent by the drivers in making daily cash collections at the five independent stores. The Court agreed that the evidence justified the differential with respect to the stores selected by the government but reversed because the record revealed that Bowman's drivers did not make cash collections from all of the independent customers who did not receive the chain-store discount. The Court remanded for further proceedings to address that issue.

The second Justice John Marshall Harlan dissented, deploring the fact that the remand would prolong litigation that had already been in the courts for nearly twelve years. He stated that if "what the record now reveals [had] been fully appreciated at the time the Jurisdictional Statement was considered, a summary disposition of the case would have been called for." He then added that "the nature of the issues in this litigation again point up the inadvisability of vesting sole appellate jurisdiction over this type of case in this Court." His point was that the statutory provision that then gave the government the right to file a direct appeal in the Supreme Court from an adverse district court decision in antitrust cases should be repealed. He reasoned that such a change would both reduce the delays occasioned by the Court's then overcrowded docket and give the Court the benefit of the court of appeals review before deciding whether to accept appellate jurisdiction. An amendment to the Judiciary Act enacted by Congress twelve years later in 1974 did make that change and thus contributed to the reduction in the size of the Court's docket today.

Justice William Douglas wrote a separate concurring opinion to stress the importance of effective enforcement of the Robinson-Patman Act's prohibition against discriminatory pricing. In his view, the act reflects "a purpose to control practices that lead to monopoly and an impoverishment of our middle class [and therefore should be read] in a way that preserves as much of our traditional free enterprise as possible. Free enterprise is not free when monopoly power is used to breed more monopoly. That is the case here unless store-by-store costs are used as the criteria for discounts."

The so-called monopoly power to which Justice Douglas referred was the power of each of the chains to switch its patronage from one dairy to another. In the trial itself, the government had not claimed that any chain or any dairy could be fairly characterized as a *monopoly,* as that word is used by economists. But Douglas's concern was not that of classical economists such as Milton Friedman; instead, it represented an approach to the antitrust laws that was characteristic of the work of the Court as a whole when Earl Warren was the chief.

In many respects I did not — and do not — agree with the approach of the Warren Court to antitrust issues. As a young lawyer, I taught courses in antitrust law at Northwestern and at the

University of Chicago. The course at Chicago, called Competition and Monopoly, was traditionally co-taught by an economist and a lawyer. The year that I substituted for Edward Levi, who later became the attorney general under President Gerald Ford and provided much-needed leadership in the Justice Department after the Watergate scandal, the economist was Aaron Director, a brilliant teacher whose disciples included Bob Bork and Dick Posner. While I did not learn half as much about economics as either of those outstanding rising scholars, I did — through my association with Aaron — pick up a few fundamentals.

For example, I learned that price concessions by competitors in free markets are more likely to benefit consumers than is rigid enforcement of rules prohibiting sellers from charging different customers different prices for similar goods. Thus, what Justice Douglas condemned as an abuse of "monopoly power" may actually have been good for the public. Similarly, the sale of one product on condition that the buyer accept another is sometimes a form of beneficial price cutting rather than an abuse of market power often condemned by characterizing it as an illegal "tying arrangement." Because Earl Warren is not noted for his antitrust opinions, I shall not attempt any in-depth review of the Court's work in that area of the law during his tenure. I shall merely state that I think many practitioners representing business clients would not have given the Warren Court high grades in a course on antitrust law.

A minor incident that occurred while I was working on the opinion in a case that was argued on my first day on the bench as a court of appeals judge may have affected my appraisal of Earl Warren's jurisprudence in cases involving economic issues. The case raised difficult questions concerning the enforceability of a National Labor Relations Board order that required the employer to engage in collective bargaining at a time when the union no longer represented a majority of the company's employees. The most relevant precedent was the then-recent forty-five-page unanimous opinion authored by Earl Warren in another labor case known as the "*Gissel* case." Because Warren's reasoning, though obviously relevant, was not directly in point, I decided that it would be helpful to examine the briefs filed by the parties in the Supreme Court. The University of Chicago Law School library then included a collection of Supreme Court briefs and records, so I was able to gain access to the briefs by visiting the law school. When I did so, I was surprised to find that Warren's opinion had copied several paragraphs from the solicitor general's brief in the case, without attribution. Needless to say, that discovery made me wonder about the care that the chief justice took, not just in writing opinions, but also in editing the work of his law clerks in cases in which he had no special interest.

Anyone interested in pursuing Warren Court jurisprudence in this area further should read the opinions in *Fortner Enterprises, Inc.* v. *United States Steel Corp.* (1969), written during the last term of Warren's tenure. The plaintiff, a real estate developer, claimed that the steel company and a wholly owned subsidiary that provided financing for the steel company's customers had engaged in a conspiracy to restrain trade in the sale of prefabricated houses. The complaint alleged that in order to obtain favorable credit terms, the defendants had forced his company to pay an unfair price for prefabricated houses. Whether such an agreement could qualify as an unlawful "tying arrangement" without proof that the defendants had monopoly power in the credit market was the subject of debate between the four dissenting justices (Harlan, Abe Fortas, Byron White, and Potter Stewart), who saw nothing wrong with the arrangement, and a majority that included Justice Douglas, who thought the answer would depend on the evidence developed at a trial. After the plaintiff had prevailed at trial and the judgment awarding damages had been affirmed by the court of appeals, the case returned to our Court. I wrote the opinion explaining our unanimous decision to reverse. That opinion not only endorsed the views expressed by the four dissenters eight years earlier but also, I believe, represented an improvement in this area of the law.

Earl Warren is entitled to high marks for his opinions interpreting the Constitution. Indeed, at least three of them represented giant strides forward on the road to the formation of a more perfect union: *Brown* v. *Board of Education* (1954), invalidating racial segregation in public schools; *Reynolds* v. *Sims* (1964), applying the "one person, one vote" rule to the election of state legislatures; and *Miranda* v. *Arizona* (1966), requiring state and local law enforcement officers to safeguard the voluntariness of confessions by prefacing their custodial interrogations of suspects with warnings comparable to those that the FBI and the British police used. Each of those opinions was a principled application of constitutional law that correctly rejected earlier precedent.

The Court heard three separate arguments in the *Brown* case. The first took place in December of 1952, when Fred Vinson was still the chief justice. After that argument, the justices were divided. There may well have been only four who were prepared to find the segregated schools unconstitutional and extend a remedy to the plaintiffs. Others, including Justice Frankfurter, were committed to dismantling segregation only gradually. Apparently Chief Justice Vinson, Justice Reed, and possibly Justice Jackson would have voted to reject the challenge to segregation. Rather than overcome these internal differences and decide the case — as it usually does after argument — the Court delayed. It ordered the parties to address several questions about the history of the drafting and ratification of the Fourteenth Amendment in a second argument in the next term. In my view, this was a mistake. The equal protection clause of the Fourteenth Amendment states a clear principle: states may not "deny to any person…the equal protection of the laws." The circumstances of its ratification cannot transform that command of equality into a license for discrimination.

Because Vinson died before the second argument was held, Earl Warren's first contact with the case occurred nearly a year after his colleagues had begun their deliberations. Over the next several months, he lobbied his new colleagues to coalesce around a single compromise position. Then, in May of 1954, he announced his unanimous opinion for the Court. On the merits, it was dead right. Warren summarily rejected as an adequate basis for decision the historical analyses that had been the principal subject of the rebriefing and reargument. Relying on a principled and correct interpretation of the equal protection clause, the Court unanimously held that state laws providing segregated public education were unconstitutional. The fact that supporters of the Fourteenth Amendment may not have intended to put an end to segregated grammar school education — or may not have realized that the amendment would do so — does not provide an acceptable reason for limiting the scope of the fundamental principle of equality embodied in the equal protection clause. The Court categorically rejected the "separate but equal" doctrine that had, as we have already seen, been silently accepted in *DeCuir* in 1878 and endorsed expressly in *Plessy* v. *Ferguson,* which in 1896 upheld a state law segregating Louisiana railcars.

Unlike most admirers of the opinion, I have never been convinced that the benefits of its unanimity outweighed what I regarded as two flaws in the Court's disposition of the cases. Instead of promptly remanding the cases to the district courts to begin the task of fashioning appropriate relief, the Court restored the cases to its argument calendar and ordered the parties to debate the proper remedy. And a year later, after considering those further arguments, the Court directed the defendants to admit the plaintiffs to public schools on a racially nondiscriminatory basis "with all deliberate speed." That belated and somewhat tentative command may have done more to encourage resistance to the clear message contained in Earl Warren's original opinion than would have a possible dissenting opinion joined by only one or two justices.

Even when a dissenting opinion makes convincing arguments on the losing party's behalf, responses by the majority may not only clarify and strengthen the Court's reasoning, but also demonstrate to the public that the dissenter's views were carefully considered before they were rejected. Moreover, as Thurgood Marshall persuasively argued, experience in Kansas and Delaware indicated that immediate desegregation was feasible. A straightforward injunction ordering the defendants to admit the plaintiffs to specific schools — like the order that the Delaware state court had entered in one of the *Brown* cases before it reached the Supreme Court — would undoubtedly have presented the trial courts with problems to be resolved on remand. But it would have lent no support to the massive resistance that developed in some states and might have pretermitted the long delays and shortfalls in desegregation that followed the Court's remedial decision. But though there may have been flaws in the remedial decision, and possibly in the Court's opinion as well, the decision represented one of the greatest achievements in the history of the Court.

The "one person, one vote" cases decided in the wake of *Reynolds v. Sims* had a profound impact on the political process throughout the country. While Chief Justice Warren is appropriately praised for that opinion, he is entitled to credit also for his earlier decision to assign the majority opinion in *Baker* v. *Carr* (1962) to Justice William Brennan. That opinion — like his later opinion in *New York Times* v. *Sullivan* (1964) — established Brennan's stature as an exceptional justice. In *Baker,* the plaintiffs had challenged the constitutionality of a Tennessee districting scheme that did not allocate representation in proportion to population; the statute gave much greater weight to votes in rural areas than to those in urban areas. Relying heavily on the Court's earlier rejection in *Colegrove* v. *Green* (1946) of a similar challenge to a 1901 Illinois statute that gave equal representation to congressional districts that varied in size from 112,000 to 900,000, the federal district court had dismissed the complaint. Justice Frankfurter's opinion in *Colegrove* included this famous admonition:

> Courts ought not to enter this political thicket. The remedy for unfairness in districting is to secure State legislatures that will apportion properly, or to invoke the ample powers of Congress.

Justice Brennan's opinion in *Baker* v. *Carr* effectively held that weighing some citizens' votes more heavily than others was a sufficiently serious violation of the equal protection clause to require judges to enter the political thicket. When one considers the extreme disparities in district sizes that cases like *Colegrove* had revealed, that conclusion was unquestionably correct. Unfortunately, however, some of the Court's later cases attempting to establish an unattainable goal of complete numerical equality have produced an even more serious threat to the political process than weighing some votes more heavily than others. As the chief justice himself observed in *Reynolds:* "Indiscriminate districting, without any regard for political subdivision or natural or historical boundary lines, may be little more than an open invitation to partisan gerrymandering."

In his dissenting opinion in *Reynolds,* Justice Harlan correctly explained that an exclusive focus on the size of electoral districts would almost certainly preclude reliance on other neutral factors and thereby produce the "indiscriminate districting" that is the breeding ground for partisan gerrymandering.

The "open invitation to partisan gerrymandering" extended in *Reynolds* was accepted by New Jersey in its reapportionment of the state's fourteen congressional districts in response to the 1980 census. All of the districts defined by the state legislature were approximately the same size — the smallest had a population of 523,798 and the largest was 527,472. The record made it quite clear that population changes during the period between the date the census was taken and the date of the election would produce greater numerical inequalities than the plan itself. In its opinion in *Karcher* v. *Daggett* (1983), the Court nevertheless held that the plan violated the principle of population equality because the state had failed to explain why it had not adopted a plan that included even lesser deviations.

I wrote a separate opinion explaining why the plan was unconstitutional for reasons unrelated to the number of voters in each district. As a glance at the map attached to the opinion demonstrates, it was an obvious gerrymander. Under our precedents condemning plans that minimize the voting strength of racial or political elements of the voting population, it violated the equal protection clause. I remain especially proud of that opinion despite the fact that none of my colleagues joined it. It relied heavily on an earlier opinion by another lonely justice — Justice Charles Whitaker, an associate justice from 1957 to 1962 — who had concluded that a racial gerrymander violated the equal protection clause two years before the Court entered the political thicket in *Baker* v. *Carr*.

In 1960, the Court unanimously held in *Gomillion* v. *Lightfoot* that the Alabama statute changing the boundaries of the city of Tuskegee "from a square to an uncouth twenty-eight-sided figure" violated the Constitution because all but a few of the African Americans who resided within the original square were outside the new city limits. No doubt recognizing the tension between that decision and Justice Frankfurter's earlier warnings about entering political thickets, the chief assigned the opinion to Frankfurter. Frankfurter tried to avoid that thicket by relying on the Fifteenth Amendment's prohibition against abridging the right to vote on account of race. But as Justice Whitaker pointed out, one person's right to vote is not abridged by a redistricting that places his residence in a different district because that person still retains his right to cast one vote, albeit within a newly assigned district. Such redistricting does, however, violate the equal protection clause if it is targeted against a racial group. In my judgment, it is equally clear that an uncouth twenty-eight-sided figure that excludes all but a few Republicans from a district in which they previously voted does so as well.

In 1966, Earl Warren wrote the opinion for the Court in *Miranda* v. *Arizona,* mandating that police provide adequate warnings to suspects in custody in order to protect both the citizen's privilege against self-incrimination and the citizen's right to counsel during custodial interrogation. Earl Warren's own extensive experience as a prosecutor must have influenced his decision in that case. Having overseen an office that obtained convictions while affording fair process to the accused, he was no doubt convinced that other professionals could do so as well. In explaining why something like the now-famous *Miranda* warnings were a necessary safeguard for American citizens, he relied heavily in his opinion on criticisms of the so-called third degree in the *1931 Report of the National Commission on Law Observance and Enforcement*, presumably sharing the opinions of the New York prosecutor quoted in the report as saying, "It is a short cut and makes the police lazy and unenterprising," and another who said, "If you use your fists you are not so likely to use your wits."

Miranda may well have been the most controversial opinion that Warren wrote during his tenure as Chief Justice. Four members of the Court — Justices Clark, Harlan, Stewart, and White — dissented because they believed that voluntary confessions should be admissible even if not preceded by warnings. A campaign to overrule the decision immediately followed. In response to that campaign Congress enacted a statute (18 U.S. Code Section 3501) that in essence provided that the admissibility of statements made during custodial interrogation should depend only on whether they were made voluntarily.

Several years later, in affirming the conviction of a bank robber named Dickerson, a federal court of appeals held that his confession was admissible under the voluntariness standard set forth in Section 3501 even though he had not received *Miranda* warnings. Dickerson sought review in the Supreme Court, claiming that the *Miranda* rule was required by the Constitution and therefore could not be changed by statute.

Before 2000, when the Court heard argument in Dickerson's case, the Court had repeatedly applied the *Miranda* rule. For example, the Court definitively reaffirmed *Miranda*'s core holding in *Rhode Island* v. *Innis* (1980), a case authored by Justice Stewart — an original *Miranda* dissenter. Stewart's effort secured join votes from Justice White, the other original *Miranda* dissenter still on the Court, and all four appointees of the president — Richard Nixon — who had campaigned in opposition to *Miranda*.

Nonetheless, strong opposition to the decision persisted until the end of the century. Although Chief Justice William Rehnquist had long been a critic of the *Miranda* decision, he wrote the Court's opinion in the *Dickerson* case that not only refused to overrule *Miranda* but also held that Congress's attempt to do so by enacting Section 3501 was unconstitutional. In explaining this position, he stated that "*Miranda* has become embedded in routine police practice to the point where the warnings have become part of our national culture."

People who enjoy watching movies that date back to the era of silent films are qualified to assess the cultural change that *Miranda* produced. In the years prior to the *Miranda* decision, it was the ham-handed, bumbling Keystone Kop that most frequently appeared in the movies; now, however, the police officer is usually and appropriately portrayed as a well-trained professional public servant. Today the typical officer is neither a bumbler nor an inquisitor who uses his fists rather than his wits.

The *Miranda* opinion unquestionably played a major role in improving the quality of police forces throughout the nation. It also, as Warren there wrote, reinforced "one over-riding thought: the constitutional foundation underlying the privilege is the respect a government — state or federal — must accord to the dignity and integrity of its citizens."

Earl Warren did not write an opinion in one of the most important cases decided during his tenure as chief justice — *Griswold* v. *Connecticut* (1965) — the case challenging the constitutionality of a Connecticut statute making the use of contraceptives a criminal offense. He must, however, accept responsibility for assigning the majority opinion to Justice Douglas, who, unfortunately, crafted an imaginative rationale for reaching an obviously correct result. Seven justices agreed that the statute was unconstitutional, and in the first paragraph of his dissent Justice Black stated that "the law is every bit as offensive to me as it is to my Brethren."

In their separate opinions concurring in the judgment, Justice Harlan and Justice White simply and correctly reasoned that the statute deprived married couples of liberty, as that concept has been used in the Fourteenth Amendment, without due process of law. They both recognized that that term does not just describe a concept that is the mirror image of the specific guarantees set forth in the first eight amendments to the Constitution, which are often described as the "Bill of Rights." Rather, as Justice Harlan put it, the "Due Process Clause of the Fourteenth Amendment stands, in my opinion, on its own bottom."

Justice Douglas's opinion is famous — or infamous — for its reliance on the proposition "that specific guarantees in the Bill of Rights have penumbras, formed by emanations from those guarantees that help give them life and substance." In his view, the statute violated the "penumbral rights of 'privacy and repose'" that earlier cases had protected. Presumably he avoided the straightforward reliance on substantive due process that Justices Harlan and White advocated because of his concern that a construction of the word *liberty* that would be broader than the specific guarantees in the Bill of Rights would rejuvenate the universally despised decision in the *Lochner* case. Unfairly, in my opinion, Justice Douglas interpreted "[o]vertones of some arguments" — presumably those of the appellants challenging the Connecticut law — as suggesting that the *Lochner* case "should be our guide." It would have been more accurate to describe those arguments as identifying a critical difference between Mr. Lochner's claimed right to freedom from regulation of his economic decisions and the kind of fundamental right that Justice Holmes identified in his *Lochner* dissent. Indeed, on pages 22 to 23 of their brief, the appellants had specifically argued that "it is vital to emphasize the difference" between legislation affecting "rights of a fundamental individual and personal character" and legislation dealing with "regulation of commercial and property rights"; they expressly stated that they were not asking for a reinstatement of the due process line of decisions exemplified by *Lochner.*

While Justice Douglas relied on the decisions in *Pierce* v. *Society of Sisters* (1925), protecting the right to educate one's children as one chooses, and *Meyer* v. *Nebraska* (1923), protecting the right to study the German language, he did so because he viewed them as consistent with the spirit of the First Amendment. In my judgment, an opinion that gives that kind of elasticity to the First Amendment is far more likely to produce unwise judge-made rules than an interpretation of the word *liberty* that protects the right to decide whether to bear children.

What I regard as the virtual incoherence in Justice Douglas's opinion in *Griswold* is no doubt attributable to his agreement with Justice Black's dissent in an earlier Fourteenth Amendment case — *Adamson* v. *California* (1947). There, Black had a different interpretation than that of Justice Harlan, who viewed the scope of the liberty that the due process clause protected as standing "on its own bottom" rather than as a mirror reflection of the first eight amendments to the Constitution. Black, by contrast, wrote that "the first section of the Fourteenth Amendment, taken as a whole" — including its guarantees of the "privileges or immunities of citizenship," freedom from deprivation "of life, liberty, or property, without due process of law," and "the equal protection of the laws" — required states to respect all of the rights identified in the first eight amendments to the Constitution. He excoriated his fellow justices for instead letting themselves "roam at will in the limitless area of their own beliefs as to reasonableness." He firmly believed that the liberty protected by the Fourteenth Amendment did not extend an inch beyond the Bill of Rights. (I remember Potter Stewart telling me that Justice Black would refuse to join any opinion that cited either *Pierce* or *Meyer*.) In later cases, the Court has firmly rejected Justice Black's rigid view.

Shortly before the end of the 1967 term of the Court, Warren attended a June 13, 1968, meeting at the White House at which he handed President Johnson a letter stating his intention to retire "effective at your pleasure." The president then nominated Associate Justice Abe Fortas to become the next chief. Fortas, however, was never confirmed because of allegations that he had both received financial benefits from a former client and acted as an adviser to the president while a member of the Court. The resulting controversy led to his departure shortly after the president's term of office expired. Thus, the resignation of Earl Warren did not become effective until confirmation of Richard Nixon's appointment of a new chief with a surprisingly similar name — Warren Earl Burger.

V

Warren Burger

Warren E. Burger, Chief Justice (1969–1986)

WARREN BURGER WAS PRESIDENT of the student council at the St. Paul, Minnesota, John A. Johnson High School, from which he graduated in 1925. In college, he sold insurance to support himself, then earned a magna cum laude degree in 1931 from St. Paul's William Mitchell College of Law. He entered private practice in Minnesota and became active in politics. He supported Harold Stassen's successful bid to be elected governor of the state, and his unsuccessful attempts to become the Republican candidate for the presidency. In 1952, when it became clear that Stassen would not be nominated, Burger reportedly led the Minnesota delegation in its decision to support Dwight Eisenhower. After becoming president, Eisenhower made Burger assistant attorney general in charge of the civil division of the Department of Justice. Three years later, the president selected him to fill a judicial vacancy on the court of appeals for the District of Columbia Circuit, where Burger served until 1969. That year, President Nixon decided to name him chief justice. He was confirmed by a vote of seventy-four to three.

I would not meet Warren Burger until three years later, during a seminar for newly appointed federal judges held at the Dolley Madison House a few blocks from the White House. Although I had been a judge on the United States Court of Appeals for the Seventh Circuit in Chicago since November of 1970, that was my first opportunity to attend such a conference.

It was a memorable event for me. I imagine that it was less so for Burger, who had by that time already written five landmark opinions and transformed how the Court handled its business.

Burger's opinion for the Court in *United States* v. *Nixon* (1974) required President Nixon to produce the tape recordings that eventually led to his resignation. The decision not only had a historic effect on American politics and society but also powerfully illustrated the integrity and independence of the Court. It may well have done more to inspire the confidence in the work of judges that is the true backbone of the rule of law than any other decision in the history of the Court.

Though not nearly as famous as the decision in *Brown* v. *Board of Education,* Warren Burger's unanimous opinion for the Court in *Reed* v. *Reed* (1971) marked the emergence of an approach to the guarantee of equal protection in the Fourteenth Amendment that would make gender-based discrimination — like race-based discrimination — constitutionally suspect. The case held that Idaho's desire to avoid hearings to resolve contests between qualified applicants for appointment to administer a decedent's estate did not justify a rule providing that the tie always go to the male applicant. The chief's brief opinion was remarkably persuasive, possibly because it avoided any elaborate analysis and simply stated that a rule mandating a preference based solely on gender was arbitrary and hence contrary to the equal protection clause of the Fourteenth Amendment. The opinion silently rejected the notion that a habitual way of thinking about different classes of equally qualified individuals provided a legitimate basis for a discriminatory rule.

The district court's orders requiring and supervising the desegregation of the schools in Charlotte, North Carolina, gave rise to several appeals, two of which produced unanimous Supreme Court opinions authored by Warren Burger. The first opinion, in *Swann* v. *Charlotte-Mecklenburg Board of Education* (1971), made it clear that district courts have broad remedial powers in segregation cases, specifically including the authority to approve busing as a remedy. In the second of those two opinions, the Court invalidated a state statute that flatly forbade assignment of any student to a particular school on account of race or for the purpose of creating a racial balance or ratio in the schools. The statute, the Court explained, impermissibly intruded upon the remedial powers of the courts. Along similar lines, the chief also pointed out that "school authorities have wide discretion in formulating school policy, and that as a matter of educational policy school authorities may well conclude that some kind of racial balance in the schools is desirable quite apart from any constitutional requirements."

While not as well known as his opinions in the Nixon tapes case, the sex-discrimination case, or the desegregation cases, Burger's opinion in *Morrissey* v. *Brewer* (1972) marked a major change in the law affecting the rights of prisoners. The case held that a convicted felon who had been released on parole — that is to say, permitted to live a normal life as long as he did not violate any of the conditions of his parole during the term of his original sentence — had a constitutionally protected interest in his conditional liberty that could not be revoked without a hearing. The case effectively repudiated the old rule that a prisoner could be treated as a slave.

Burger's opinion in *Morrissey* provided the basis for the opinion that I wrote for the court of appeals in *United States ex rel. Miller* v. *Twomey* (1973), which held that a prisoner's good-time credits were also protected from arbitrary cancelation. As I shall explain, that opinion provided the basis for my response to questions posed to me by Senator Edward Kennedy during my confirmation hearings.

Notwithstanding the significance of these five early Burger writings, it was another set of Burger's achievements preceding my tenure on the Court that foreshadowed his signal contribution to American law: improvements to the administration of justice within and beyond the Court. While Earl Warren had been interested in deploying American-style rule of law abroad to achieve world peace, Warren Burger concentrated on improving the administration of that legal system domestically in both federal and state courts. He was thus a strong supporter of the work of the Federal Judicial Center that Congress had authorized in 1967 to provide education and assistance to federal judges. The creation of the National Center for State Courts, in 1971, was also largely due to his efforts. His interest in the center's educational programs remained high in subsequent years.

Even more active in administrative matters at the Supreme Court itself, Burger made changes that have had a lasting effect on its work. One of the most obvious — though often forgotten today — was the change in the shape of the bench that took place during the winter recess of the October 1971 term. What was formerly a straight bench, which prevented most of the justices from seeing any colleagues other than their immediate neighbors, was angled in three sections. As a result, all nine justices can now see and hear one another as well as the advocates. Whereas the two most junior justices — seated at opposite ends of the bench — once had great difficulty hearing exchanges, now all nine members of the Court have equal access to one another as well as to the advocate.

Each justice has access to one of the pages sitting behind the bench on seats that are not visible to most people in the courtroom. The justices normally have the written briefs in the case being argued on the bench with them, but they also each have two pads of paper. One, a blank pad, is for notes that a page will deliver to a colleague at the other end of the bench or occasionally to a guest of a justice in the audience. The second pad contains forms on which the justice may request the page to obtain a specific court opinion. Most such requests are for previous Supreme Court opinions gathered in the volumes shelved in the area immediately behind curtains that are opened when the justices ascend the bench. Prompt responses to requests for books in the library on the third floor are possible because that area is served by a book elevator. Promptness is important because requests are usually motivated by an interest in either checking the accuracy of a statement made by counsel or a colleague or providing the basis for propounding questions to counsel.

Other equipment available to the justice but not visible to the audience includes a water pitcher, a goblet, writing materials, a drawer (in which I kept a pocket-size copy of the Constitution), and a toggle switch to turn on the microphone when the justice starts to ask a question. By long-standing tradition each justice also has a metal spittoon next to his or her chair; I have never seen anyone make use of that elegant remnant of tradition.

When the microphones are turned off, a justice will occasionally exchange a comment or two with his immediate neighbor. For most of our careers, Nino Scalia and I sat next to each other, and I was the beneficiary of his wonderfully spontaneous sense of humor. One morning when we heard a case involving a defendant who had refused to answer questions about the crime under investigation but volunteered a long incriminating statement about a more serious offense and a second case in which the defendant had refused to sign a written confession while verbally describing inculpatory facts in great detail, Nino whispered to me that this must be our "dumb defendant day."

On another occasion many years ago, while listening to an inept argument, Potter Stewart, who had a powerful bass voice and was sitting on the other side of Lewis Powell, my immediate neighbor, failed to turn off his microphone before intoning in what he intended to be a whisper: "Where did this guy come from?" I'm sure his booming voice was heard throughout the courtroom.

I believe Burger was the primary person responsible for a change in the rules governing oral arguments that has had lasting significance. Oral arguments matter because they are often the first time that the justices speak with one another concerning the merits of the case. While it is often said that a lawyer can lose but cannot win a case at oral argument, I view that dichotomy as misleading. Lawyers seek to highlight key points for the justices and, equally important, assist the justices as they discuss the case among themselves. Thus, it is the one time when lawyers and justices labor together in the same room, albeit not always collaboratively, on the work of the Court.

When Burger joined the Court, the rules authorized two hours for oral arguments, with each side having a full hour. While the Court occasionally placed cases on the summary docket, which allowed each party only thirty minutes, on July 1, 1970, the Court implemented its present rule limiting the time for each advocate to thirty minutes in all cases. The primary concern motivating that change was the overcrowded condition of the docket that then required afternoon sessions on every argument day. (Because the Court's shrinking docket has meant that that concern no longer exists and because several justices now consume so much time asking leading questions, it would make sense for them to take a second look at that rule.)

While Burger spent the years before our first meeting working on landmark cases and improving the administration of American justice, I supplemented the last few years of my practice with a different kind of high-minded pursuit: I learned to pilot a single-engine plane and began flying on a regular basis. In 1968 I paid $10,500 to become the proud owner of a one-year-old Cessna 172 with the call sign 1688 F. During the two summers before I became a judge, I commuted between my second home in Michigan and Meigs Field on the lakefront of Chicago in eight-eight foxtrot. The change in my employment when I became a judge in 1970 involved a cut in pay that made it necessary to sell the Michigan house, but I kept the plane, which I used on weekends.

Coincidentally, Robert Sprecher, who also left private practice when he became the junior judge on the court of appeals a few months after I did, found it necessary to sell his summer home in Fox Lake, Illinois, when he became a judge. The fact that the salaries of federal judges are significantly lower than the market value

Group photograph of Court of Appeals for the Seventh Circuit (1975).

Seated from left: Judge Luther Swygert, Senior Judge John Hastings, Chief Judge Thomas Fairchild, Senior Judge Latham Castle, and Judge Walter J. Cummings. Standing from left: Judge Philip W. Tone, Judge John Paul Stevens, Judge Wilbur Pell, Judge Robert Sprecher, and Judge William Bauer. *Used with permission of the United States Court of Appeals for the Seventh Circuit.*

of their services as practicing lawyers has prevented many qualified lawyers from accepting the opportunity to perform judicial
service. But because I have always enjoyed and been gratified by
the opportunity to serve as a federal judge, I have never regretted
my career change.

On one Saturday I flew to DePauw, Indiana, to hear Harry
Blackmun give the commencement speech at his daughter's graduation. After his talk, I introduced myself, explaining that I had
been recently appointed to the Seventh Circuit by President
Nixon. Early the next week, Bob Sprecher, who had joined the
court shortly after I had, received a gracious letter from Harry
saying how nice it was to have met him at DePauw. Years later,
after I became a colleague of Harry's, I enjoyed recounting that
event as evidence of (a) what a nice guy Harry was, and (b) his
having, despite his reputation for meticulous accuracy in all of
his work, in fact made at least one mistake.

My Cessna also provides one of the two reasons for remembering the significance of my first meeting with Warren Burger.
The meeting occurred shortly after I landed at Dulles International Airport, completing my first solo flight to a destination
from which I could not return to Chicago on the same day. The
second reason is that it gave me an opportunity to talk to the
chief about the unanimous opinion he had recently announced
in *Groppi* v. *Leslie,* a case in which a Catholic priest had challenged the constitutionality of a resolution adopted by the Wisconsin legislature. Groppi had led a parade protesting cuts in
welfare payments onto the floor of the general assembly and publicly stated to his cheering supporters that they had captured the
capitol and intended to stay until the legislature restored funds

for welfare recipients. Their occupation of the assembly lasted from approximately midday to well near midnight. Thereafter, the protesters were kept out of the state capitol building by police, sheriffs, and the National Guard. Those facts would seem to provide ample support for bringing charges against Groppi. But rather than allowing a prosecutor to initiate criminal proceedings, the legislature instead took the unusual step two days later of adopting a resolution finding Father Groppi guilty of contempt and sentencing him to prison. In its opinion denying Groppi's petition for habeas corpus, the Wisconsin Supreme Court — a well-respected state court composed of elected judges — had taken judicial notice of facts reported in the press.

Nevertheless, Jim Doyle, the federal district judge sitting in Madison, granted Groppi's petition for habeas corpus after Groppi brought suit before him to challenge his confinement. Doyle reasoned that even though there were rare situations in which a legislature might hold a party in contempt, the Groppi resolution was flawed because it was adopted without giving him any notice or affording him an opportunity to present a defense or information in mitigation. A few days before I was sworn in as a judge, a Seventh Circuit panel composed of three excellent judges — John Hastings, Walter Cummings, and Wilbur Pell — reversed Judge Doyle, concluding that no hearing was necessary because the contemptuous conduct had occurred in the presence of the legislators who had adopted the resolution.

A few days after I was sworn in as a circuit judge, John Hastings, who had been appointed by President Eisenhower and had served as the chief judge of the circuit court, paid me a visit and we had the first of many conversations about the court, our experiences as practicing lawyers, and the law. When he was the chief judge, he had attended a number of judicial conferences in Washington at which Earl Warren had presided. While John was not an admirer of Warren's jurisprudence, he had high praise for the way he chaired judicial meetings and for his friendly personality.

Discussing his own approach to judicial work, John told me that he always wrote the first draft of his opinions (as opposed to having a clerk do so) because, as he explained, if you write a complete and accurate statement of the facts, "the rest of the opinion will write itself." In later years, he expressed concern that, as he grew older, he might not realize that the quality of his work was declining, and he asked me to promise that I would tell him if I thought that was happening. I never had to do so, but I had that conversation in mind when I obtained a similar commitment from Justice David Souter regarding my own work many years later. When John passed away in 1977, I flew to Washington, Indiana, in eight-eight foxtrot to attend his funeral.

In my initial conversation with John Hastings, he made a comment about the Groppi case. I think Groppi may have already filed a petition for an en banc rehearing — a request that the case be reargued in a hearing before all eight of the active judges on the court — before our conversation took place. John did not discuss the merits of the case, but I vividly remember one remark that he made. He said that he had asked Wilbur Pell, who had recently been appointed to the Court by President Nixon, to write the opinion because it was the kind of case that might be noticed in Washington. One of the themes of Nixon's presidential campaign had been a promise to appoint "law and order" judges who would follow the law rather than engage in the kind of "activism" that he ascribed to Earl Warren.

Of the seven voting judges, a majority of four — Luther Swygert, Roger Kiley, Otto Kerner, and I — voted to rehear the case en banc. Judge Hastings had been ineligible to vote to rehear the case en banc because he was a senior judge, but as a member of the original three-judge panel, he was allowed to vote on the merits once it was taken en banc. After the reargument, Judge Kerner joined Judge Hastings in the majority to vote to uphold the contempt conviction. I wrote a dissent that Judges Swygert and Kiley joined. That dissent may well have been my most significant court of appeals opinion because I thought that it put an end to any possibility that I might be considered for appointment to the Supreme Court.

I really do not believe that the remote chance of my being appointed to a higher court would actually have affected any of the decisions that I thereafter made. But just as the quality of the work of all federal judges is enhanced by the guarantee of life tenure that enables them to put an interest in popularity to one side when they are seeking the answers to difficult questions of law, what I assumed to be a complete removal of any possibility of advancement insulated my further work on the court of appeals from any such distracting influence.

When I met Chief Justice Burger after he had announced the opinion upholding my dissenting views, I was looking forward to his comments on the case. His opinion for a unanimous Court, after all, had not only reversed an en banc decision of our court of appeals but also rejected the reasoning in a unanimous opinion of the Wisconsin Supreme Court. In my view, the difference between the federal and state courts' appraisals of this highly visible case may well have been affected by the fact that the Wisconsin judges were elected by the voters whereas Chief Justice Burger and his colleagues enjoyed life tenure.

In my conversation with the chief, I did not learn whether he shared that view. He was most gracious during our brief meeting — as he was with all the other new judges at the conference — but he was obviously unaware of my dissent. He seemed not even to realize that the case had arisen in the Seventh Circuit.

While Burger may not have given any special thought to whether conscious or subconscious concerns about possible public reaction to a high-visibility case might affect the quality of a judge's work, for me the Groppi case has been an ever-present reminder of the critical difference between the work of a judge and the work of other public officials. In our democracy, issues of policy are determined by majority vote; it is the business of legislators and executives to be popular. But in litigation, judges have an overriding duty to be impartial and to be indifferent to popularity. Sir Matthew Hale, a respected English judge, described an essential attribute of judicial office in words that have retained their integrity for centuries:

> 11. That popular or court applause, or distaste, have no influence upon any thing that I do in point of distribution of justice.
>
> 12. That I not be solicitous of what men will say or think, so long as I keep myself exactly according to the rules of justice.

Thinking about Groppi, I quoted those words in a speech to the Chicago Bar Association in 1974 in which I opposed both the popular election of judges and making a judge's continued tenure depend on the outcome of a periodic retention ballot. While I have always considered financing a campaign and soliciting votes unseemly for judicial candidates, I am even more troubled by the potential impact on the work of the judge of allowing popularity to be treated as an appropriate criterion for determining his or her fitness for office. An important reason for respecting the quality of the work that federal judges perform day in and day out is our confidence in their independence.

My real relationship with Chief Justice Warren Burger began in 1975 in the period after President Ford nominated me to fill the vacancy caused by Justice Douglas's resignation and before I was confirmed by the Senate some nineteen days later. While neither the White House nor the Department of Justice did anything to prepare me for the Senate hearings, they did arrange a series of meetings with individual senators.

I enjoyed those meetings immensely, learning what should have been perfectly obvious, that men (and they were all men) who are popular enough to win statewide elections are generally very good company. I particularly enjoyed my conversation with Senator Barry Goldwater, not just because he had been a candidate for the presidency in 1964 but also, and more important, because he was a pilot who enjoyed talking about the various military aircraft that he had flown. I received the impression that he decided to vote for me when he learned that I had my own plane.

The purpose of my meetings with individual senators was to avoid a repetition of the unfortunate failure to confirm the nomination of Judge Clement Haynsworth, a fine judge who was well qualified for service on the Supreme Court. Questions had been raised about Haynsworth's failure to disqualify himself in one or two cases in which he had participated as an appellate judge. Some of the senators whom I met in 1975 told me that they had voted against him because they thought his answers to questions posed at his hearings had been evasive but had later learned that he had a speech defect that often gave listeners an incorrect impression about his candor. To avoid mistakes of that nature, the senators had decided to arrange informal meetings with nominees. In my case, those meetings were primarily social occasions devoid of discussion about substantive legal issues.

My meeting with Senator Strom Thurmond of South Carolina was an exception. After he introduced me to his entire staff, he asked me to come into his office for a private discussion. He began by stating: "Judge Stevens, I want to talk to you about the death penalty." I was prepared to tell him about an important opinion that I had written as a circuit judge to explain why I thought I should not discuss my views on that issue, but it was unnecessary for me to do so because he immediately continued: "I am not going to ask you for your opinion — for that would be improper — but I want to tell you how I feel about it." He then made a perfectly reasonable explanation of why he thought the death penalty played an important role in effective law enforcement. He said nothing that he would not have said in a public setting. A similar scenario occurred during my later meeting with Senator McClellan of Arkansas. After I met with Senator Edward Kennedy of Massachusetts, a member of his staff presented me with a copy of a book that E. Barrett Prettyman Jr. had written arguing that capital cases have an adverse impact on the orderly development of the law.

I think that it was during my visit to Washington to meet senators that Warren Burger invited me to have lunch with him in his chambers. I had never been in the chief's chambers when I served as a law clerk. They include three of the five rooms in the area immediately behind — though across the hall from — the courtroom. His principal office is behind the reception area where his secretaries work and is also adjacent to the large room (the conference room) where the justices conduct their discussions about Court business and assemble before going on the bench. On the opposite side of the conference room, the chief has a second office where he may work in private. The fifth room in the area (the robing room) contains the lockers where the justices' robes are stored and donned and doffed. It was in the chief's principal office that his messenger served us our lunch.

Although I had been told that he had urged the president to nominate Clifford Wallace, an excellent judge on the Ninth Circuit, to fill the vacancy, he could not have extended a more friendly welcome to me than he did. My principal memory of that luncheon is my feeling of awe and disbelief in finding myself back in the building where I had had such a wonderful job as a law clerk. While I later learned that the shape of the bench had been changed and that the justices' chambers — which had all been located in the eastern half of the ground floor when I was a clerk — had been enlarged to include more space on the first floor as well as significant space on the second floor, in my perception, the building was exactly the same as I remembered. I do not recall receiving any advice from the chief about how to prepare for the hearings other than his observation that the Court would benefit from prompt action by the Senate because a vacancy impaired the ability of the Court to handle its workload efficiently. Harry Blackmun did, however, provide me with a copy of the hearings conducted by the Judiciary Committee before he was confirmed, so I had fair notice of what to expect. My principal adviser was Ed Rothschild, my former partner. He came to Washington with me and helped me respond to the burdensome requests for information about our practice, about possible conflicts of interest in cases that I had heard as a circuit judge, and other inquiries about my health and financial resources.

The senators were particularly concerned about the state of my health as a fifty-five-year-old nominee because I had recently had heart surgery performed by Dr. Norman Shumway at Stanford University Hospital. Ed and I provided them with all the available details about my physical condition, but we were more concerned about potential questioning about the death penalty and the opposition to my nomination by the National Organization of Women (NOW). With regard to the former, we agreed that it would be appropriate to decline to answer such questions; I had not sat on a capital case, so any views I might have expressed would have necessarily been tentative and potentially misleading because competent counsel might raise arguments that I had not considered. Moreover, my comments might have been misconstrued as commitments, which I, of course, could not properly make. We decided that I should explain my refusal by referring to a novel case in which I had participated in 1972.

As it turned out, I did not have to discuss the case, but since it sheds some light on Warren Burger's evolving jurisprudence, I shall describe it. A new Republican secretary of state of Illinois had discharged many non–civil service employees hired by his Democratic predecessor. The plaintiffs — who had held jobs as janitors, clerical workers, license examiners, and the like — alleged that they had been discharged because they refused to become Republicans and to support the Republican Party. Because the case was dismissed in advance of trial on the grounds that the employees had not alleged a violation of any federal right, the appeal presented the legal question whether such non-policy-making employees could be discharged for refusing to transfer their allegiance from one political party to another.

When I first looked at the papers, I was happy to have such an easy case to decide. Like my colleagues on the panel, I thought it obvious that patronage practices that enabled newly elected officials to reward their supporters by providing them with public jobs had long been entrenched in American history and must be constitutional. But after argument and further study, I came to the conclusion that even though "the patronage system is defended in the name of democratic tradition, its paternalistic impact on the political process is actually at war with the deeper traditions of democracy embodied in the First Amendment." In 1976, the Supreme Court, over a dissent by Justice Powell, which the chief joined, endorsed that conclusion. In 1980 the chief joined my opinion for the Court in *Branti* v. *Finkel,* a case holding that two assistant public defenders were protected from discharge based on their political beliefs.

While Ed and I were less concerned about the opposition by NOW than about potential questioning seeking my views about the death penalty, we did correctly anticipate some questioning about gender-based discrimination. I had written an opinion for a three-judge district court holding that a majority vote in the Illinois House of Representatives did not qualify as a vote to ratify the Equal Rights Amendment because state law required a three-fifths majority vote; I had also written an opinion arguing that an airline's policy of hiring only unmarried flight attendants did not unlawfully discriminate against women because the airline had another rule making men ineligible for the position. Since a person of the opposite sex would have been treated less favorably, it did not seem to me that the challenged rule discriminated against females. The test that I applied in that case, and in later cases after I joined the Court, was whether a plaintiff claiming unlawful class-based discrimination would have been better off if he or she had been a member of the favored class.

As it turned out, the senators did not ask me about either of those cases, but they did ask me whether I favored the adoption of the Equal Rights Amendment. While I knew that my answer would not be helpful to my cause, I explained that I thought the proposed amendment should not be adopted because the equal protection clause of the Fourteenth Amendment, as construed by Warren Burger's opinion in the *Reed* case, already provided women with adequate constitutional protection against gender-based discrimination.

Formal group photograph of the 1975 Burger Court.

Seated from left: Justices Byron R. White and William J. Brennan Jr., Chief Justice Warren E. Burger, and Justices Potter Stewart and Thurgood Marshall. Standing from left: Justices William H. Rehnquist, Harry A. Blackmun, Lewis F. Powell Jr., and John Paul Stevens. January 1976. *Photograph by Robert Oakes, National Geographic, Courtesy of the Supreme Court of the United States.*

In his questions and comments, Senator Edward Kennedy seemed more concerned about my qualifications than any of his colleagues were. He wondered whether there was anything in my record to indicate that I would be fair to claims asserted on behalf of underprivileged citizens. It was another Warren Burger opinion that enabled me to respond effectively to that line of questioning. Burger's opinion requiring a hearing before a prisoner's parole could be revoked provided the centerpiece for one of the most important opinions that I had written as a circuit judge — *United States ex rel. Miller* v. *Twomey* (1973) — a case arising out of prison disciplinary proceedings. So when Senator Kennedy asked me for evidence that members of what he described as those with "submerged aspirations" would benefit from my confirmation, I was able to produce two letters from inmates in the Illinois state prison that expressed their support for me.

On the third day of the hearings, Senator James Eastland of Mississippi, the chairman of the Senate Judiciary Committee, took action that convinced me that he would vote for me. A hostile witness — who was claiming that I acted dishonorably in 1967 as counsel to a commission investigating the integrity of an Illinois Supreme Court decision — was reading a long prepared statement when the senator quietly asked me if I wanted to listen or reply to his testimony. When I said no, he told the court reporter to make a full record of the witness's statement, and, while the witness's diatribe continued, we left the hearing to share a little bourbon in his office. The statement of the witness is quoted in full in the transcript of the hearings; what Senator Eastland and I had to say in his office was — and shall remain — off the record.

While members of the executive branch did not help Ed and me prepare for the Senate confirmation hearings, they did provide us with a car and a driver who picked us up at our hotel and took us to the Capitol in the morning and then back to our hotel at the end of the day—with one exception: when the hearings ended, we were on our own and had to hail a cab.

The majestic courtroom in which the Court hears oral arguments and the justices announce their opinions is located on what is considered the first floor of the building. The clerk's office, a cafeteria, a motion picture theater, the statue of John Marshall, portraits of former justices, and a kiosk where souvenirs and books are sold are located on the ground floor. On an even lower level there is a large garage, the police headquarters, and other offices. Occupants of the second floor today include Justice Sonia Sotomayor and her four clerks; about half of the law clerks who are appointed by and work for other justices; the official reporter of decisions, who oversees the final editing and printing of all opinions; and the computer experts who play a vital role in maintaining the efficiency of the writing and communications facilities available to everyone else. The library is on the third floor, the gym on the fourth, and there is storage space on those floors as well. Except for Sonia and David Souter—who no longer keeps an office at the Court—all of the active justices, as well as the retired justices, now have their main chambers on the first floor.

When I was one of a total of fifteen law clerks in 1947, the chambers of all nine justices, including space for clerks, secretaries, and messengers, were located on the first floor in the east half of the building. The chambers were adjacent to one another, forming a large U surrounding the courtroom. The main entrance to the Court is on the west side of the building. To pass from there to the courtroom and on to the chambers to the south, east, and north involves traversing the extremely spacious great hall, the sides of which are lined by busts of former chief justices. In 1947 Justices Jackson and Burton had a view of the lawn to the north; Justice Black had the northeast corner office; Justice Frankfurter, Chief Justice Vinson, and my boss, Justice Rutledge, looked out on the buildings across Second Street to the east; Justice Reed had the southeast corner office; and Justices Murphy and Douglas had a view of the Library of Congress to the south. None of them could look out the window and see either the Capitol, which is directly across the street to the west of the Court, or the flight of marble steps that ascends from the plaza outside the Court two stories up to the main entrance. The conference room, where the justices meet to make their decisions, was then, as now, in the center of the back (east) side of the building, adjacent to the chief's office.

Whereas my most vivid memory of my first oral argument on the court of appeals is the friendly handshakes with Luther Swygert and Roger Kiley, what I remember most clearly about the first argument I heard as a Supreme Court justice is how I approached and left my seat on the bench. The approach identified a five/four division among the nine members of the Court; the exit reflected my respect for Lewis Powell, who sat next to me.

Seniority determines where each of the nine justices sit. The chief has the center seat, the senior associate sits on his right, the next most senior on his left, and so on. When the marshal shouts, "Oyez, oyez" (the traditional equivalent of "Hear ye, hear ye"; it is pronounced "Oh yay," not "Oh yez"), and requests all of the spectators in the courtroom to rise, the justices ascend the bench in groups of three: the chief justice and the two most senior justices are in the center; the fourth, sixth, and eighth most senior justices enter at the right end of the bench; the fifth, seventh, and ninth most senior justices enter at the left end. Thus, using numbers to describe the lineup in the conference just prior to entering the courtroom, the sequence is 123-468-579.

The five-four split that impressed me on my first day was that of the five justices who were over six feet tall and the four — Justices Brennan, Stewart, Blackmun, and Stevens — who were all within an inch or two of five feet six. As the most junior, I was at the end of the line, with the six-foot Lewis Powell (number 7) in front of me, and the even taller Bill Rehnquist (number 8) in front of him. The only other justices visible to me were the broad-shouldered Thurgood Marshall (number 5), the all-pro running back Byron White (number 4), and our handsome leading man (number 1). I won't say that I felt insignificant, but I did feel that I was beginning my tenure as a member of a small minority.

During the argument, Lewis Powell carefully explained that when we adjourned I should be sure to push my chair back far enough to enable Thurgood and himself to walk past it before descending the steps from the bench. At the end of the argument, attentive to that counsel, I gave my chair such a firm shove that I missed catapulting down those stairs by only a matter of inches. I continue to thank the good Lord for saving me from what would have been a truly memorable opening argument.

Though in 1975 I was the most junior justice and Burger was the chief, we were equals with respect to the most important duty and privilege involved in our work: casting votes and expressing views about how cases should be decided. Becoming the junior justice after the Court has heard arguments in over sixty cases is somewhat like leaping onto a moving train after it has left the station and is still gaining speed. At the time of my arrival at the Court, it seemed that every one of my new colleagues was busily engaged in drafting, criticizing, and rewriting portions of the 294 pages of opinions that were announced on January 30, 1976, in the famous campaign finance case known as *Buckley* v. *Valeo*. While I did not participate in the case, because it had been argued before I arrived, I was provided with copies of the seemingly endless parade of writings that my new colleagues circulated. Because I thought that I should keep abreast of the ongoing debate, my principal memory of my first weeks on the Court is one of extreme distaste for debates about campaign financing. That distaste never abated, and I have felt ever since that the Court would be best served by inserting itself into campaign finance debates with less frequency. That view may have had an impact on the unusually long dissent that I wrote during my last term on the Court against the Court's overreaching in the *Citizens United* case — a case in which the Court essentially rewrote the law relating to campaign expenditures by for-profit corporations and unions in order to decide that a wealthy nonprofit corporation could use its assets to televise and promote a movie about Hillary Clinton wherever and whenever it wanted.

In addition to my overriding hostile reaction to the subjects discussed in *Buckley,* I also recall puzzlement about why the Court failed to endorse the position expressed by Justice White in his dissent. He effectively explained why the distinction between limitations on contributions (which the Court upheld) and the limitations on expenditures (which the Court invalidated) did not make much sense, and why the Court should have respected the congressional judgment that effective campaigns could be conducted within the limits established by the statute. Time has vindicated his prediction that without "limits on total expenditures, campaign costs will inevitably and endlessly escalate." He thought it quite proper for Congress to limit the amount of money that a candidate or his family could spend on a campaign in order "to discourage any notion that the outcome of elections is primarily a function of money."

The majority's response to Justice White relied on the rhetorical flourish that "the concept that government may restrict the speech of some elements of our society in order to enhance the relative voice of others is wholly foreign to the First Amendment." The assumption underlying that colorful argument is that limitations on the quantity of speech in public debates are just as obnoxious as limitations on the content of what a speaker has to say. But there is nothing even arguably unfair about evenhanded rules that limit the amount of speech that can be voiced in certain times or places or by certain means, such as sound trucks. If we view an election as a species of debate between two adversaries, equalizing the amount of time (or money) that each can spend in an attempt to persuade the decision-makers is fully consistent with the First Amendment. Otherwise, appellate court rules limiting the time that the adversaries spend in oral arguments would be invalid because they limit the speech of one adversary in order to enhance the relative voice of his or her opponent.

*   *   *

While I was still digesting the circulations in the *Buckley* case, the chief provided me with copies of the pool memos that had been prepared for upcoming conferences, and he invited me to join the pool. Those memos were a response to the problems presented by the need to process the voluminous papers filed by litigants asking the Court to review the decisions of federal and state courts that had ruled against them. In Warren Burger's first term as chief, 3,435 such filings arrived, more than double the number filed in Earl Warren's first term.

Before I joined the Court, Justice Lewis Powell had suggested that a great deal of valuable time could be saved by having a clerk prepare a memorandum for each application, summarizing it and recommending an appropriate disposition. The chief and Justices Byron White, Harry Blackmun, and William Rehnquist agreed with Lewis's suggestion, and their clerks formed a pool whose work products those justices shared.

I found the sample pool memos to be extremely thorough summaries of the parties' filings, but based on my earlier experience as a law clerk, I was convinced that in most cases I could make an accurate judgment about whether to grant or deny the petition more easily by glancing at the original papers than by reading an unnecessarily detailed description of the arguments favoring and opposing review. I therefore declined the chief's invitation to join the pool. Before making that decision I did not discuss the matter with any other justice, but I do recall a later conversation with Justice Stewart in which he expressed a favorable reaction to my decision because he thought the pool should not include more than five justices. While I have never had second thoughts about staying out of the pool, my refusal may not have been the most diplomatic decision that a new member of the Court could have made. I was, however, joined in my abstinence by Justices Brennan, Stewart, and Marshall.

Early in that term, the chief initiated a conversation with me about *National League of Cities* v. *Usery* (1976) — a case that presented the question whether the Constitution permitted Congress to require states to pay their employees federally mandated minimum wages. I think that was the only case whose merits the chief and I discussed before argument. A majority of justices on the Court ultimately held that Congress did not have the challenged power. Bill Brennan wrote a powerful dissent in that case, but because he used such strong language — referring to the majority's "catastrophic judicial body blow at Congress' power under the Commerce Clause" — I decided to write a brief dissent of my own. While I have since concluded that Justice Brennan's rhetoric was entirely appropriate, I think my dissent, coupled with my refusal to join the pool, may well have affected the chief's appraisal of his most junior colleague. Despite his possible disappointment, though, I never felt that the chief treated me unfairly when making opinion assignments — or, indeed, in any other respect.

The only way in which Burger changed my responsibilities as a junior justice from those who had preceded or would succeed me was by not asking me to testify at congressional hearings to review the Court's budget proposals. I was happy to avoid that responsibility. It also probably explains why I have never known as much about the financial operation of the Court as my colleagues. I am the only former justice appointed after Burger became chief whose sole appearance at a congressional hearing came while being considered for confirmation.

The junior justice on the Court has a variety of other duties, most of which were ones to which I acclimated quickly. I remain confident that I was competent in my performance of two in particular. One was the product of long-standing tradition. The second was a by-product of Warren Burger's leadership. It is the job of the junior justice to get up and open the door if anyone knocks while a conference is being held. I did commit one unforgivable error in my first or second conference: I was so absorbed in the discussion that I did not realize that someone had knocked until Bill Brennan on my left and Bill Rehnquist on my right pushed back their chairs and got up to answer the door. That humiliating lesson taught me to keep track of priorities — for the junior justice, there is one responsibility even more important than being fully informed about the views of your colleagues: remembering that you are what Tom Clark described as the most highly paid doorman in the country.

That incident reminds me of my favorite way of explaining my vote when I was the last to speak after four of my seniors had voted to reverse, and four had voted to affirm. Because Brennan and Rehnquist were invariably on opposite sides of such cases, I liked to begin by announcing: "I agree with Bill."

From what I have been told, I understand that Warren Burger is responsible for another unique task now performed by the junior justice. Apparently, before Harry Blackmun came aboard, the chief justice noted the decisions made by the Court on petitions for certiorari and similar matters and later reported those actions to the clerk of the court for announcement on the official order list, which was then published on the following Monday. Harry — who, as I have noted, had a deserved reputation for meticulous accuracy — observed on more than one occasion that the clerk's announcements did not correspond with his own notes. When Harry advised the conference that the chief was not an entirely reliable note-taker, apparently everyone agreed that Harry should undertake that task; it has been performed by the junior justice ever since. I hope I am correct in remembering that I performed it with the skill and reliability of a Harry Blackmun.

The chief, rather than the junior justice, was responsible for one significant nonjudicial aspect of our conferences. As a regular part of the proceedings, we would have a midmorning coffee break that lasted for at least fifteen or twenty minutes. It was the chief's responsibility not only to be sure that coffee and tea were promptly served but also to select the menu, an assortment of pastries and fruits. More important, he personally dunned each of his colleagues for the ten-dollar contribution he collected every few weeks to finance our extravagant tastes. We often took those breaks after voting on one of the argued cases, and an informal understanding that usually — but not always — prevailed during those breaks was that we would suspend discussion of legal issues.

In my judgment, Warren Burger's contributions to the law in the years after I joined the Court have not been fully appreciated, possibly because unfriendly critics have had so much to say about Burger's evolving views about the abortion issue. Public interest in that issue increased dramatically in the years after 1973, when

Roe v. *Wade* was decided. As the seven-to-two vote in that case illustrates, the basic issue was not as controversial in 1973 as it became in later years. Indeed, in 1975 when the Senate Committee on the Judiciary held hearings on my nomination to the Court, no senator asked me a single question about abortion. And, as Justice Clarence Thomas confirmed during his hearings in 1991, he had not encountered debates over the case among his fellow students when he was attending Yale Law School.

The debate that did develop in later years may, in part, have been fostered by the difference between Justice Blackmun's opinion for the Court and Justice Stewart's more straightforward analysis in his concurring opinion. While Blackmun's thorough discussion of history and the evolving views of the medical profession merit careful study, and his explanation of why the word *person* as used in the Fourteenth Amendment does not include the unborn effectively ended the debate on that issue, I think it unfortunate that his legal reasoning placed so much emphasis on a so-called right of privacy protected by "penumbras of the Bill of Rights."

Far more persuasive was Justice Stewart's explanation that the *Griswold* decision that had upheld the right to use contraceptives could "be rationally understood only as a holding that the Connecticut statute substantively invaded the 'liberty' that is protected by the Due Process Clause of the Fourteenth Amendment." In his view, cases protecting the right of the individual, whether married or single, to be free from unwarranted governmental intrusion into matters so fundamentally affecting a person as the decision of whether to bear or beget a child necessarily included the right of a woman to decide whether to terminate her pregnancy. He found it "difficult to imagine a more complete abridgment of a constitutional freedom than that worked by the inflexible criminal statute now in force in Texas."

Neither Justice White's nor Justice Rehnquist's dissenting opinion disagreed with the Court's explanation that an unborn fetus is not a "person" entitled to constitutional protection. Both of them objected primarily to the breadth of the Court's protection of "abortions performed during the first trimester of pregnancy."

The importance of the capital punishment cases decided by the Burger Court is well known. That Warren Burger and Harry Blackmun, who voted to uphold the constitutionality of the death penalty, both opposed it as a matter of policy is less well known. The chief has also seldom been given the credit he deserves for his opinion in *Lockett* v. *Ohio* (1978). That case involved a challenge to her death sentence by a woman who had been the getaway driver in an armed robbery during which one of her accomplices had shot and killed a victim. Under Ohio law, the sentencer had been unable to consider such potentially mitigating factors as the defendant's "character, prior record, age, lack of specific intent to cause death, and her relatively minor part in the crime." Burger's opinion reversing the challenged death sentence recognized the rights of capital defendants to introduce all mitigating evidence relevant to the punishment issue. That opinion continues to play a major role in every capital sentencing proceeding in the United States.

Two other significant opinions that Warren Burger authored after I joined the Court have interesting histories. My favorite is the so-called snail darter case, in which the court of appeals held that the Endangered Species Act required it to enjoin the operation of the virtually completed Tellico Dam and Reservoir Project on the Little Tennessee River to save an endangered species from extinction. In the spring of 1977, when the acting solicitor general filed a petition seeking review of that order, my law clerk Dan Farber (who has since had a distinguished career as a law professor) wrote me a memo stating, in part, that the "arguments made in the [petition] are so feeble that it is surprising that the SG's office was willing to take the appeal."

The Court took no action on the petition that spring, but we did discuss the case at our conference in September before the opening of the term. Not sharing Dan's appraisal of the case, four justices — the chief, Byron White, Lewis Powell, and Bill Rehnquist — then or shortly thereafter thought the court of appeals was so clearly wrong that its decision should be reversed without the Court's even hearing argument. Harry Blackmun cast a vote known as a "join three," meaning that he would cast the fourth vote to grant review if three others voted that way. The case was then relisted for Bill Rehnquist, which meant that no decision on the matter would be reached until a future conference on the understanding that he would prepare an opinion reversing the Sixth Circuit. During the first week in October, Bill circulated such a draft, and Potter Stewart and I each responded with draft dissenting opinions. Lewis Powell then weighed in with an opinion that used a different line of analysis to reach Rehnquist's result. After reviewing the opposing drafts, Blackmun circulated a memo stating that his preference was that the conference grant certiorari; three other justices joined him in voting to do this soon thereafter.

Normally it is the solicitor general or one of his or her assistants who represents the government in oral arguments in the Supreme Court, but there is also a tradition that at least one such argument should be made by the attorney general. Following that tradition, Griffin Bell presented the argument on behalf of the Tennessee Valley Authority contending that the public interest would be served by completing the dam notwithstanding the language in the Endangered Species Act on which the lower court had relied. The main point that he made was that the snail darter was not a species of any great importance — certainly not one that justified the refusal to complete the dam on which millions of dollars had already been spent. To emphasize that, he brought with him a small glass jar containing a snail darter. His argument was unpersuasive; indeed, at our conference on the merits, Byron White voted with those of us who had been in favor of affirming the court of appeals judgment from the beginning. According to my notes, the chief was equivocal during voting, but he apparently remembered differently or changed his mind, for soon thereafter he assigned the majority opinion to himself. The excellent opinion that he then wrote explained why the investment in the dam was less important than obeying a congressional command to protect the snail darter. He closed with a quotation of words attributed to Sir Thomas More about the importance of the rule of law:

> The law, Roper, the law. I know what's legal, not what's right. And I'll stick to what's legal....I'm *not* God. The currents and eddies of right and wrong, which you find

such plain-sailing, I can't navigate, I'm no voyager. But in the thickets of the law, oh there I'm a forester....What would you do? Cut a great road through the law to get after the Devil?...And when the last law was down, and the Devil was turned round on you — where would you hide, Roper, the laws all being flat?...This country's planted thick with laws from coast to coast — Man's laws, not God's — and if you cut them down...d'you really think you could stand upright in the winds that would blow then?...Yes, I'd give the Devil benefit of law, for my own safety's sake.

Partly because of its quality and partly because of its history, it is one of my favorite opinions.

Five years later Burger wrote a unanimous opinion in a case in which a Florida trial judge had divested a divorced mother of the custody of her three-year-old daughter because her new partner, whom she later married, was an African American. The Florida Court of Appeals had affirmed the order without opinion, and in February of 1983, the mother filed an application for a stay in our Court, seeking to maintain the status quo pending our review of the case. In my view, she had a strong case: the child had been in her custody for three years, there was no question about her fitness as a parent, and her argument that the race of her new partner did not provide a constitutionally acceptable basis for giving her ex-husband custody of the child was a strong one. On March 7, the Court entered an order denying the stay application. Volume 460 of the official United States Report, at page 1018, correctly states that I voted to grant the stay, but my own notes reflect that after our conference, Thurgood circulated a memo changing his vote to a grant. Neither my notes nor the official report contains any explanation for the majority's decision.

We did not act on the mother's petition for certiorari until after the summer recess, but at our conference on October 14, 1983, four of us — Bill Brennan, Thurgood, Harry Blackmun, and I — voted to grant review; the case was argued in February of 1984 and decided in April. During that period of more than a year, the order giving the father custody remained in effect.

Warren Burger's lucid five-page opinion concluded with this statement:

> Whatever problems racially mixed households may pose for children in 1984 can no more support a denial of constitutional rights than could the stresses that residential integration was thought to entail in 1917. The effects of racial prejudice, however real, cannot justify a racial classification removing an infant child from the custody of its natural mother found to be an appropriate person to have such custody.

The reasoning in his opinion explains why the mother's application for a stay should have been granted. I suppose the Court reached its proper conclusion "with all deliberate speed," but I continue to regret its failure to act more promptly.

In 1983 Burger made two significant contributions to First Amendment law. In that year, John Anderson ran as an independent candidate for president and challenged the constitutionality of an Ohio statute that required him to meet a March filing date in order to have his name on the ballot. The chief provided the critical fifth vote backing my opinion in *Anderson* v. *Celebrezze* (1983) giving greater weight to the associational rights of his supporters than to the interests in protecting the two-party system from competition. In 1983 Burger also joined my opinion in *Branti* v. *Finkel,* which, as I noted before, held that the Constitution protects assistant public defenders from being discharged solely because of their political beliefs.

It was in 1980 that the chief's repeatedly stated views about the limited reach of the Second Amendment gained voice in Justice Blackmun's opinion for the Court in *Lewis* v. *United States.* Warren Burger particularly enjoyed conversations about the history of the Constitution — indeed, his eventual decision to resign from his position as chief justice was motivated by his desire to provide appropriate leadership in the celebration of the bicentennial of the Constitution. On a good many occasions he went out of his way to criticize scholars who argued in favor of a broader reading of the Second Amendment. Although none of his colleagues shared his rather emotional reaction, I never heard anyone on the Court express any disagreement with his views about the Second Amendment. And in *Lewis,* Blackmun wrote on behalf of the Court that "the Second Amendment guarantees no right to keep and bear a firearm that does not have 'some reasonable relationship to the preservation or efficiency of a well regulated militia.'" That uncontroversial statement remained an accurate characterization of the Court's long-settled and correct understanding of the meaning of the Second Amendment up until the Court's unfortunate decision in *District of Columbia* v. *Heller* (2008), in which the Court held that the Second Amendment protects the right of individuals to keep a handgun in the home.

As I have already mentioned, Burger used his position as chief justice of the United States to improve the administration of justice throughout the nation. At the Court, this effort led to many improvements as well as to some changes that I do not think were for the best. One area where Burger unquestionably made a positive difference was in securing and developing the heritage of the Court.

Warren Burger was a great admirer of Chief Justice John Marshall. (I think he gave greater deference to Marshall's rulings as a trial judge in the famous case against the former vice president Aaron Burr than he did to opinions of the entire Court.) Consistent with this admiration, he succeeded in having the Court acquire possession of the statue of John Marshall that had previously been located outdoors on Capitol Hill.

Ronald Reagan's inauguration as president was what made the acquisition possible. Prior to that event, presidential inauguration ceremonies had been conducted on the east side of the Capitol; the Marshall statue was located on the west side, where, of course, it was not visible to observers of the ceremony. When Burger learned that Reagan's 1981 inauguration would break with tradition and be held on the Capitol's west side, Burger requested that the statue of John Marshall be moved to a new home inside the Supreme Court. That request was approved, and the statue was moved to its present location on the ground floor of the Court. In the intervening years, the statue has reminded the thousands of tourists who visit the Court each year of the important role that the great chief justice played in our history. For those particularly familiar with the history of the Court, the statue has special significance as the work of the sculptor William Wetmore Story, who was the son of Justice Joseph Story. Justice Story not only served with Marshall but also was one of our greatest justices.

It is also thanks to Chief Justice Burger that since 1972 the mahogany chair from which Chief Justice John Marshall presided over the Court is the seat that each new justice takes during the investiture ceremony. Whether or not members of the audience are impressed by that detail, I can testify without fear of contradiction that every one of us who sat in that chair as our presidentially signed commission was read in open court will never forget the experience.

Burger showed special respect for Marshall and the history of the institution that he led in other ways as well. He is entitled to credit for creating the position of curator of the Court and for organizing the Supreme Court Historical Society. That society regularly publishes scholarly articles in its periodical, sponsors important research about the early documentary history of the Court, and operates the kiosk. And to help the chief perform the nonjudicial responsibilities that I described in the second chapter of this book, Burger persuaded Congress to authorize the appointment of an administrative assistant for that purpose.

Burger obtained portraits of both of the litigants in the famous case of *Marbury* v. *Madison* and had them hung in the small dining room on the second floor. When only a few members of the Court are present for lunch, instead of using the regular justices' dining room, they frequently decide that the Marbury v. Madison room will provide a better setting for friendly conversation. Normally, when the justices lunch together in either of those adjacent rooms, the conversation does not include any discussion of Court business. That is one of the traditions that preserve the genuine collegiality among the members of the Court.

A similar tradition that Burger initiated and that his successors have faithfully followed may have been inspired by his being a connoisseur of fine wines. Before every justice's birthday that occurred when the Court was in session, he sent around a note announcing the date when we should all be sure to be present at the lunch in the justices' dining room on the second floor to celebrate the occasion. He provided the wine that was used for the toast that preceded the singing of "Happy Birthday"; the rendition was always enthusiastic and heartfelt, even if the harmony left much to be desired. Like the practice of shaking hands with every member of the Court before going on the bench to hear oral argument, that custom played an important role in maintaining the cordial relations among the nine individuals who sometimes used pretty strong language when expressing disagreement with the views of the majority on more important issues.

I think Warren Burger is also entitled to credit for several improvements in the Court's procedures and machinery that provide significant savings in the scarce time of busy justices. Three involve changes to the Court's rules. These include the rule imposing maximum limits on the number of pages in the parties' briefs, the rule requiring that the question presented by a petition for certiorari be set forth on its first page, and the rule prescribing the colors of the covers of the different categories of printed documents that the parties file. For example, a petition seeking review via certiorari will have a white cover, the response an orange one, and any reply to the response a tan one. If the Court grants the case, the parties then submit merits briefs. The petitioner's brief has a light blue cover, that of the respondent has a red cover, and any reply comes in yellow. Interested nonparticipants, known as amicus curiae — that is, friends of the court — also often submit briefs. Amicus briefs filed before the Court decides whether to hear a case have cream-colored covers; those filed after the Court grants review are green — dark green if they support the petitioner, and light green if they support the respondent. And whenever the United States files a brief, it uses a gray cover. Being able to recognize instantly that, say, the red brief is the respondent's brief on the merits may save only a few seconds each time a justice or a clerk looks for it, but the total time saved as a result of the rule is enormous.

Chief Justice Burger's leadership in introducing electronic word processing into the routine work of the Court also resulted in unquestionable benefits. The change, along with the consequent closing of the print shop, has saved justices and their staffs countless hours in performing their routine duties. The risk that the Court will be unable to adjourn until well into July — as happened in my first term as an associate justice — is now virtually nonexistent.

Perhaps the contrast between the pre-Burger and post-Burger technologies is best illustrated by noting another technological advance. Before Burger, the Xerox machine was unknown to the Court.

It has always been my judgment that Warren Burger was an excellent presiding officer during oral arguments. He was courteous and fair to counsel. He did not hesitate to allow a lawyer a few extra minutes when questioning from the bench had taken up so much time that the advocate had not had a fair opportunity to make his or her argument.

Burger was not, however, equally proficient as a presiding officer at our conferences. Four shortcomings are worthy of note. His introductory description of the issues in an argued case was sometimes incomplete or more fairly described as a statement of his own views about the case. Perhaps for that reason, either Bill Brennan or Potter Stewart would often introduce his own presentation with a neutral statement of the issues before commenting on the merits. Potter was particularly skillful in summarizing complexities in simple, lucid language; he was unusually brilliant and articulate.

On occasion, instead of waiting until each of his eight colleagues had spoken, the chief would interrupt the discussion to add a point he had omitted or even to repeat a point that had already been made. He was less well prepared, and less articulate, than either of the men who held the position after him.

Based on conversations that I have had with former clerks of Chief Justice Warren, I understand that Warren followed the same practice with regard to the order of voting that Chief Justice Vinson had — namely, after introductory comments were made in order of seniority, the most junior justice was the first to vote, and the chief was the last. Warren Burger must have been responsible for what I regard as an unfortunate reversal in the order of voting.

Of greater importance, in cases presenting multiple issues, he did not always take accurate notes about the views expressed by each of his colleagues on each issue. For that reason, there were cases in which he assigned the majority opinion to a justice whose views on one or more issues did not command a majority. There were also occasions on which he assigned the majority notwithstanding his own continuing uncertainty about the proper disposition of the case. The better practice — followed by his successors — would have allowed the next senior justice in the majority to make the assignment. An assignment that he made to me in my first term on the Court illustrates the sometimes tentative character of the views he expressed at conference.

Buffalo Forge Co. v. *Steelworkers* (1976) presented the question whether a federal court could enjoin a union from engaging in a sympathy strike that was expressly forbidden by the union's collective bargaining agreement. At our conference in March, five of us — the chief, Bill Brennan, Harry Blackmun, Lewis Powell, and I — voted in favor of the employer's position that the no-strike clause was enforceable even before the dispute had been arbitrated. The chief assigned the majority opinion to me, and Byron White stated that he would write a dissent.

After I circulated my draft, Thurgood Marshall changed his vote and joined my opinion. While that welcome letter led me to believe that I would have six votes supporting my opinion, Harry Blackmun responded with a letter stating that after reading my draft he had changed his mind and planned to join Byron's dissent. Finally the chief circulated a note advising us that although he favored my result, he had concluded that it required action by Congress, and therefore he was joining Byron, which made the vote five to four in Byron's favor. In the next few days Byron and I redrafted our respective opinions so that the case could be announced on July 6.

Perhaps that sequence of events proves merely that Byron was more persuasive than I. It was, however, also consistent with friendly advice that Potter Stewart gave me in a conversation shortly after I joined the Court. He said, in substance, that the author of a Court opinion should always keep in mind the possibility that either the chief or Harry, or possibly both, might not adhere to the position expressed at conference.

Of course, there are a fair number of cases in which some justices disagree with the majority at the conference after oral argument but ultimately are persuaded to join its opinion. Byron White, on occasion, concluded that an issue was not sufficiently important to justify the preparation of a dissenting opinion; he referred to his reluctant join in such a case as a "graveyard dissent." Some of our greatest justices followed that practice many years ago. In my judgment, however, the institution and the public are better served by an accurate disclosure of the views of all of the justices in every argued case.

I can recall — with some pride — announcing at least two significant unanimous opinions in cases in which the Court had originally been divided at its conference. In my first term, we heard reargument in *Mathews* v. *Diaz* (1976), a case involving the welfare rights of alien residents. The eight justices who had heard the argument the term before had been equally divided; they eventually all joined my majority opinion upholding a federal requirement that aliens have five years of continuous stateside residence and be admitted to permanent residence in order to participate in a federal medical insurance program. And in the most frequently cited opinion that I ever wrote — *Chevron U.S.A. Inc.* v. *Natural Resources Defense Council, Inc.* (1984), a case in which we held that the court of appeals should have accepted the administrative agency's interpretation of an ambiguous provision in the statute — Byron White had assigned the opinion to me because both the chief and Bill Brennan had voted the other way. After I circulated my draft majority, the chief joined without comment but Bill raised a question about my reading of the statute. I visited his chambers to discuss the point with him and his law clerk Michael Klausner (who is now a professor at Stanford Law School). After our meeting, I think he joined my draft without requiring any changes.

I also disagreed with the chief on a matter of writing conventions. This became clear during a tea I shared with Burger in his office. When the chief wanted to discuss a controversial matter with a colleague, he would often extend an invitation for that colleague to have a cup of tea with him in his chambers. On the occasion in question, he and I discussed the use of the word *we* in Court opinions. I found the issue particularly interesting because I had had a similar discussion with Tom Fairchild when he was the chief judge of the Court of Appeals for the Seventh Circuit. On that court, I had written a few opinions in which I made it clear that my vote was based on stare decisis — the doctrine that judges should adhere to rules announced in earlier cases — rather than on my own views about the issue. Tom had persuaded me that the law would be better served by using the word *we* to confirm the fact that the court was a continuing body bound by stare decisis regardless of our individual views.

Warren Burger took a different view. He suggested that a new justice needed at least two years to become comfortable in dealing with the awesome responsibilities that membership on the Court entailed. Moreover, he argued, it was not accurate to use the word *we* to describe a group of judges that did not include the author. There is no doubt some merit to the view he expressed. I do not share it because I remain persuaded that the most junior justice is just as much an equal of the chief as their seven other colleagues.

Another expression of that equality is on the matter of disagreements. As far as I know, all the justices with whom I served agreed that each of us had an equal right to disagree publicly. The junior justice has the same right to announce a dissent in an oral statement in open court as does any other justice, including the chief. In a conversation shortly after I joined the Court, Potter Stewart told me that John Harlan had more than once expressed the view that in every term, at least one dissenter should announce his opinion from the bench. He thought that such announcements revealed qualities of some of our disagreements that could not be adequately expressed in writing. I have repeated that conversation to most, if not all, of my newer colleagues, and the custom has been preserved.

In some instances, the cases that the Court decided touched upon and even transformed the procedures through which the Court conducted its business. A small example of this phenomenon was *United States* v. *Grace,* a 1983 case in which we upheld the constitutionality of the statute that prohibits certain public demonstrations in the Supreme Court Building and on its grounds except insofar as it included the surrounding sidewalks. Supreme Court police officers responsible for enforcing the statute have long encountered a myriad variety of protesters. For instance, Mary Grace, one of the plaintiffs in the case, carried a four-by-two-and-a-half-foot sign on which the text of the First Amendment was written. On another occasion, a protester wore a large wooden sandwich board on which random spatterings of illegible hieroglyphics were inscribed. When the officer asked him what they meant, the demonstrator firmly responded, "That's a secret."

When Mary Grace filed her lawsuit in the federal district court, she named Warren Burger as the principal defendant. When the court of appeals held that she was entitled to relief, the caption of its opinion was "Grace v. Burger." Our opinion upholding the statute except insofar as it applied to the sidewalks omitted any discussion of whether it was proper for the chief — or, indeed, for any of the rest of us — to participate in the decision. I remember the chief vigorously expressing his view that a litigant should not be allowed to disqualify an impartial judge by unnecessarily naming him as a party to a case. I think our discussion of the disqualification question reflected a consensus that either all of us or none of us should participate. It would have been wiser for our opinion to describe that consensus because Burger, as the named party, was unfairly singled out for criticism for not disqualifying himself.

A more significant case that was also decided in 1983 led to a major change in the work of the Supreme Court. In earlier years, the Court's review of state criminal cases had almost always been a response to a claim by the defendant that his federal constitutional rights had been violated. If a state court afforded the individual greater protection than the federal constitution required, there was no need for federal intervention. It had always been the law that a state legislature or a state constitutional provision could grant its citizens rights that federal law did not mandate. The fact that a state court decision rested on both a state and a federal ground generally provided a sufficient justification for the Supreme Court's refusal to hear the case.

The Court reversed its presumption against review of state overenforcement of federal constitutional rights in *Michigan* v. *Long*. There, the Court held that it was proper to review such cases unless the state court made it clear that there was no federal issue to be decided by including in its opinion an unambiguous statement that its decision rested on an adequate and independent state rule. That decision essentially invited petitions from prosecutors claiming that a state court had granted too much protection to one of its citizens.

The impact of a judicial approach that places greater weight on obtaining uniformity among the state courts in their rulings on federal questions than on making sure that federal rights are adequately protected is illustrated by another opinion announced on the same day. The California Supreme Court had held, correctly, in my view, that a jury instruction in a capital case violated the federal Constitution because it tilted the scales in favor of imposing the death penalty in close cases. The instruction informed the jury that the governor had the power to commute a life sentence without the possibility of parole but failed to inform them that he could also commute a death sentence. A bare majority of the justices on our Court held that the instruction was permissible as a matter of federal law and sent the case back to the state court to decide whether it violated the California constitution. On remand, not surprisingly, the state court again invalidated the instruction but this time it supported that result by relying on its own constitution rather than the federal Constitution. It thus reached the same result that about twenty-five other states had reached by relying on their own state rules. The case illustrated how far out of step the five members of this Court's majority were and, more important, the triviality of the benefits to be derived from expanding the Court's power to review state court decisions supported by reliance on both federal and state rules.

When that case was decided, the Court was already overworked. It was hearing oral argument and writing full opinions in about a hundred and fifty cases each term. Serious proposals, some initiated by Chief Justice Burger, considered the advisability of creating an intermediate court of appeals to process certiorari petitions. Some critics, including Justice White, thought that the Court was not adequately performing its duty to resolve important conflicts in the lower courts on questions of federal law and therefore should grant cert more frequently. My own view was the exact opposite. I agreed that it would be wise to cut back on the Court's mandatory jurisdiction but that we were granting an unnecessarily large number of certiorari petitions. I particularly opposed reviewing state court decisions like the California jury instruction case in which the only issue was whether state judges had granted their citizens greater protection than federal law required. The burdens associated with hearing too many cases persisted throughout Warren Burger's tenure as chief. In my judgment, those burdens should be characterized as "self-inflicted wounds," not just because of their impact on our workload but also because prosecutors seemed to prevail more often than defendants. As the *Chicago Tribune* cartoon reproduced here indicates, those decisions adversely affected the public's perception of the Court as an impartial guardian of the rule of law.

Chicago Tribune cartoon by Jeff McNelly (April 1984). *Used with permission of the Chicago Tribune.*

Discussion of one final procedural change under way during Burger's tenure will help to introduce the means by which he brought his tenure as chief justice to a close. The Supreme Court reviews cases pursuant to its "mandatory jurisdiction" and "discretionary jurisdiction." The former describes those lower court decisions that Congress has by statute required the Supreme Court to hear. At one time, the Supreme Court decided many such cases. The case that I argued in 1962 was such an appeal. As a result of amendments eliminating most of the Court's mandatory jurisdiction, only a few such appeals are now heard each year. In the vast majority of the cases presented to the Court, a losing litigant has filed a petition for certiorari invoking the discretionary jurisdiction of the Court. The denial of such a petition permits the decision of the lower court to remain in effect, but it does not constitute a ruling on the merits by the Supreme Court. Most of the orders entered by the Court are denials of certiorari that merely inform the parties that the Court will not hear their case.

When the Court does grant certiorari, the parties must file briefs and make oral arguments addressing the merits. Afterward, the Court needs time to prepare the opinions explaining its decision. Frequently, during the months that elapse between a grant of certiorari in a case and announcement of a decision on the merits, other petitions will be filed raising either the same issue or an issue that may be affected by the ruling in the case under advisement. It is the practice of the Court to hold such petitions on the docket until the pending case is decided. Following the announcement of an opinion in the pending case, an appropriate order is entered in every held case — usually either an order denying certiorari review or an order remanding the held case to the lower court for reconsideration in the light of the just-announced opinion.

On the final day of each term, after the last opinions have been announced, the justices return to the conference room to dispose of the cases that have been held pending the announcement of those opinions and to decide any other matters that need attention. It was at such an end-of-term conference that Potter Stewart (in 1981) and Lewis Powell (in 1987) informed his colleagues (other than the chief) of his decision to retire. I remember an especial sadness on both of those occasions — and in Lewis's case, a few tears shed by Potter's successor, Sandra Day O'Connor.

Warren Burger's decision to retire was unusual in two ways. First, it broke from the mold described above. On June 17, 1986, well before the end of the Court's term, he sent a letter to President Reagan requesting that he "be relieved as Chief Justice of the United States effective July 10, 1986, or as soon thereafter as my successor is qualified." In proceeding in this way, he was something of a trendsetter; like Burger, I later announced my own retirement in a letter to the president sent well before the end of the term. Burger, however, gave a unique reason for stepping down. He explained that in his position as chairman of the Commission on the Bicentennial of the Constitution, he was responsible for telling the story of our great constitutional system to the American people and that telling "that story as it should be told is an enormous and challenging task" that he could not adequately perform while continuing in his judicial office.

It was several weeks later that I learned of his decision and sent him a note expressing my disappointment. His response, which alluded to his leaving his office at about one thirty in the morning, confirmed his estimate of the burdens of his work on the Bicentennial and his appraisal of the importance of that assignment. It was, of course, also important to the Court because it led to the president's nomination of William Hubbs Rehnquist as the sixteenth chief justice of the United States and, because Rehnquist had to give up his seat as an associate justice to become chief, of Antonin Scalia's appointment as the 103rd justice of the Supreme Court.

VI

William Rehnquist

William H. Rehnquist, Associate Justice (1972–1986), Chief Justice (1986–2005)

B ILL REHNQUIST WAS A meteorologist in the Air Force during World War II. After the war, he studied law at Stanford University, graduating at the top of his class and securing a clerkship with Justice Robert Jackson. Jackson was clearly one of the Court's most gifted writers — for example, in his opinion endorsing Chief Justice Stone's position in the flag salute case, he wrote:

> If there is any fixed star in our constitutional constellation, it is that no official, high or petty, can prescribe what shall be orthodox in politics, nationalism, religion, or other matters of opinion or force citizens to confess by word or act their faith therein.

Nevertheless, his dissent in the *Bob-Lo* case and his decision to leave the Court to act as a prosecutor in the Nuremberg trials prevent me from ranking him among our greatest justices.

After his clerkship with Jackson, Bill and his wife, Nan, decided — based in part on a meteorologist's expert appraisal of the favorable climate in Arizona — to settle in Phoenix, where Bill practiced in a small firm.

In 1969, he returned to Washington to head the Office of Legal Counsel to the president. Two years later, President Nixon selected him to fill the vacancy on the Court created by the second Justice Harlan's resignation.

Bill had served as an associate justice for fourteen years when President Reagan chose him, in 1986, to be the chief justice. In the Senate, a substantial number of legislators opposed his confirmation because they regarded his opinions as reflecting insensitivity to civil rights issues. That opposition overlooked the fact that the change in his status from an associate justice to chief justice would not give him any additional voting power. Because of the senators' concentration on the qualifications of Rehnquist, they devoted relatively little attention to the far more important question of what kind of justice the new appointee, Antonin Scalia, would be. He, of course, was exceptionally well qualified and would have been confirmed overwhelmingly even if he had been the center of attention. Nonetheless, there is irony in the fact that the senators were far more interested in raising questions about Rehnquist than they were in questioning the new justice.

The vote to confirm Rehnquist was a lukewarm sixty-five to thirty-three. His colleagues on the Court, however, welcomed him into his new position. We all regarded him as a friend who we knew would handle his new responsibilities competently and impartially. He more than fulfilled that expectation throughout his career as chief justice.

Like many chief justices, Bill first presided over his colleagues in person at the initial conference of the term in which he held his new position. It is at that conference that the Court acts on the large volume of petitions for certiorari and jurisdictional statements that have accumulated during the summer recess. Before I joined the Court, the conference was held during the week that started on the first Monday of October, when the new term began. A few years before Bill became chief, however, the

Court accepted Harry Blackmun's suggestion that the conference occur in September so that oral arguments could begin on the first day of the new term. Bill's maiden appearance thus came a week earlier in the year than had those of his predecessors.

Presumably because at sixty-two he was younger than most of his colleagues, Bill suggested at the conference that we continue to call him by his first name. We promptly and unanimously rejected that suggestion. While we are informal in our communications with one another, the tradition of addressing the first among the nine equals as either Chief or, occasionally, Mr. Chief Justice is firmly embedded in our procedures. (The latter term will no doubt be shortened to Chief Justice as soon as a woman occupies that office.)

That the change in our chief would change the tenor of our deliberations was clear from the outset. Under Warren Burger's leadership, the opening conference usually ended some time on Wednesday. On the first day of Bill's leadership, I think we completed our work shortly after Monday's lunch. That type of efficiency characterized all of Bill's work as chief. At our conferences on argued cases, he insisted that each of us speak only in turn, and he protested additional debate or discussion after the first round of comments was completed. He was equally firm in those protests regardless of whether the speaker agreed or disagreed with his own views. In short, he was a totally impartial presiding officer.

Moreover, he was meticulously accurate in noting and remembering the different positions advocated by different justices on each issue presented in each argued case. To the best of my memory, he never assigned a majority opinion to a justice whose views were not supported by at least five votes in the conference discussion. Of course, there were occasions when further study persuaded a justice to change his or her mind, but such changes were not attributable to any defect in Bill's leadership.

Efficiency and impartiality also characterized his leadership in oral arguments. On an argument day, a buzzer sounds in each justice's chambers at 9:55 a.m. Argument is scheduled for 10:00. In the intervening five minutes, the justices must arrive in the robing room, don their robes, and then greet one another with handshakes either in that room or in the adjacent conference room, where they must line up in time to make their entrance into the courtroom. Inevitably, handshakes breed conversations, both in the robing room and in the conference room. These impede preparation for the timely parade that enables three groups of three justices each to ascend the bench simultaneously in response to the marshal's cry of "Oyez, oyez." As chief, Rehnquist was ever mindful of threats to punctuality in the timing of our entrance. His careful herding ensured that we entered the courtroom at precisely 10:00 every time. I am quite sure that he surpassed all his predecessors in supervising and guaranteeing justices' "on-time arrivals."

He was equally vigilant in making sure that every oral argument ended on time. A white light on the lectern warns the advocate that his or her time will expire in five minutes, and a red light signals the end of the allotted time. When Chief Justice Rehnquist was presiding, the moment the red light went on, the argument was over. He sometimes interrupted an advocate in the middle of a sentence and rarely (if ever) allowed anyone any extra time.

As was true of his conduct at our private conferences, he was totally impartial when presiding in open court, holding veterans such as the solicitor general of the United States to exactly the same strict time limits as younger lawyers making their first arguments. Thus, when Senator Arlen Specter, later the chairman of the Senate Judiciary Committee, was presenting his oral argument challenging the legality of the closing of military installations in his state and attempted to add a few words after his time expired, he was summarily rebuffed. (In subsequent conversations that I had with the senator in the barbershop of the Senate Office Building and elsewhere, he made it quite clear that he well remembered that rebuff.)

Although he was informal with his colleagues, the chief thought it important that lawyers address members of the Court as Justice rather than Judge, and there were occasions when he reminded a lawyer that he was the chief justice. The reminder, of course, was not necessary. In addition to sitting in the middle of the bench and presiding over arguments, Bill had affixed four gold stripes on each sleeve of his robes. Any observer could tell that he held a unique position among the nine of us. His decision to embellish his robes with those stripes came as a surprise to the rest of us. He had previously described his favorable impression of the colorful robes worn by some judges at an international conference that he had attended and suggested that we consider a change in our attire. We had immediately and uniformly given him a negative response to that suggestion. Nevertheless, with regard to his own robes, he went right ahead.

Efficiency also characterized Bill's preparation of opinions. When he was an associate justice, the Court was confronted with the question whether President Reagan's executive order providing for the arbitration of disputes between the Iranian government and American businesses was constitutional. A prompt answer to the question by our Court was essential to maintaining American credibility in this sensitive area of foreign relations, for the order helped implement the agreement that had led to the release of the American hostages taken in Iran in 1979. No doubt because of his confidence in Bill's ability to craft an acceptable opinion promptly, Warren Burger assigned him the Court opinion. Despite the complexities and the novelty of the issues, it took Bill only a matter of days to complete a draft upholding the executive order, which all of us joined.

As chief justice, he set an example for the rest of the Court by completing all of his own opinion assignments promptly. I understand that he enforced a ten-day rule that accorded his clerks only that limited period in which to complete the first draft of every one of his opinions. No matter how large the record was or how difficult the legal issues were, the draft was due in ten days. I think the quality of some of his opinions may have been adversely affected by that rule. As is apparent from what I have written in numerous dissents — such as my opinion in the *National League of Cities* case, which I have already mentioned, and in Justice David Souter's and my dissents in the *Seminole Tribe* case, which I will discuss shortly — I consider the quality of the writing far less important than the quality of the judgment that many of those opinions revealed.

Bill enjoyed gambling for modest stakes. He and I bet a dollar on virtually every Redskin game. I usually lost because I tended to bet on the home team. When Bill lost, he always paid his debt as soon as we met on Monday morning. He would also organize betting pools during elections, during the Kentucky Derby, and sometimes to predict the depth of accumulating snow in areas adjacent to the Court.

Rehnquist enjoyed preparing for the term-end party, which included skits written and performed by clerks and a *Jeopardy!*-type quiz for which he drafted questions about the history of the Court and a variety of obscure topics. He might ask the names of litigants in cases decided during the term or the name of a Confederate general who fought in a particular Civil War battle; he might ask for a list of the pairs of justices who shared the same name. (If you count Justices John Clarke and Tom Clark and also count Owen Roberts and Rehnquist's immediate successor, John Roberts, there are ten. The other eight pairs are Samuel and Salmon Chase, the first and second John Marshall Harlans, Howell and Robert Jackson, Thomas and William Johnson, Lucius and Joseph Lamar, John and Thurgood Marshall, John and Wiley Rutledge, and Edward and Byron White.)

Rehnquist liked to sing, knew the lyrics of many songs, and could recite from memory a variety of familiar poems, including John Greenleaf Whittier's "Barbara Frietchie," which he quoted in full in his dissent from the holding in *Texas* v. *Johnson* that the First Amendment protects flag burners. An excerpt from that poem reads:

> *On that pleasant morn of the early fall*
> *When Lee marched over the mountain wall, —*
>
> *Over the mountains winding down,*
> *Horse and foot, into Frederick town.*

Forty flags with their silver stars,
Forty flags with their crimson bars,

Flapped in the morning wind: the sun
Of noon looked down, and saw not one.

Up rose old Barbara Frietchie then,
Bowed with her fourscore years and ten;

Bravest of all in Frederick town,
She took up the flag the men hauled down;

In her attic-window the staff she set,
To show that one heart was loyal yet.

Up the street came the rebel tread,
Stonewall Jackson riding ahead.

Under his slouched hat left and right
He glanced: the old flag met his sight.

"Halt!" — the dust-brown ranks stood fast.
"Fire!" — out blazed the rifle-blast.

It shivered the window, pane and sash;
It rent the banner with seam and gash.

Quick, as it fell, from the broken staff
Dame Barbara snatched the silken scarf;

She leaned far out on the window-sill,
And shook it forth with a royal will.

"Shoot, if you must, this old gray head,
But spare your country's flag," she said.

A shade of sadness, a blush of shame,
Over the face of the leader came;

The nobler nature within him stirred
To life at that woman's deed and word;

"Who touches a hair of yon gray head
Dies like a dog! March on!" he said.

Although I did not tell Bill at the time, my concern that this lengthy quotation might detract from the force of the legal analysis in his opinion was one of the reasons that I decided to write my own dissent.

In most cases, Bill led guests at the year-end party in group singing, accompanied by Judge Edward Becker of the United States Court of Appeals for the Third Circuit, who regularly made the trip from Philadelphia to play the piano for us.

As our weekly football-season wagers reflect, Bill liked sporting events. Basketball was his particular favorite, at least while his son was a star on his high school team. I am told that Bill sometimes used rather strong language to voice his disapproval of unfavorable rulings by the referee in his son's games. With regard to his colleagues, he used somewhat milder language, though it was still emphatic. He often described the harsh consequences of his strict enforcement of a rule that seemed inequitable to some of us as "tough tacos." Bill had a good sense of humor, but unlike some of his colleagues, he seldom displayed it at oral arguments.

Bill also liked playing sports, though he had a bad back that sometimes was painful and limited his ability to exercise. He went swimming almost every day and also played a good deal of tennis. He had a weekly game with his law clerks and required the best of the three to play as his partner. I suspect that his pre-hiring interviews enabled him to field a winning team every year. On weekends he occasionally played doubles at his country club in Virginia. He received prescription medication for the pain in his back, and there was a brief period — well before he became chief, I believe — when his taking that medication affected his speech, though I never thought that there was any impact on his ability to work efficiently.

My wife, Maryan, and I have especially fond memories of Nan Rehnquist, Bill's wife. At some time during Earl Warren's tenure, the spouses of the justices began to hold three or four luncheons each year. Typically they rotated the roles of the hostesses, with three of them taking responsibility for selecting and preparing the menu for each luncheon. Widows of deceased justices and wives of retired justices were treated as equals in both planning and attendance. Originally known as the wives' luncheon, the occasion became the spouses' luncheon after Justice O'Connor joined the Court. Her husband, John, attended frequently, but unlike Ruth Ginsburg's husband, Marty, he did not play a leading role in planning or hosting the lunches that he attended. There seems to be a consensus, however, that Marty was one of the most talented chefs ever to take part in those affairs.

The luncheon is held on the ground floor of the Supreme Court Building in a three-room suite that includes a dining room, a parlor, and a kitchen. That area was called the wives' dining room, and then became the spouses' dining room, and is now the Nan Rehnquist Room. The spouses chose that name because of their uniformly deep affection for Bill's wife. She died, a victim of cancer, during the fifth year of Bill's tenure as chief. I have nothing other than the most favorable memories of Nan. She was an extraordinarily gracious and friendly person.

Though Rehnquist ran a tight ship as chief without losing the goodwill of his colleagues, it is as the equal of other members of the Court — in deciding cases — that he had his greatest impact. In some areas, like separation of powers, he and I found common ground. The basic contours of that concept are well known. The people of the United States ordained and established the Constitution in order to form a "more perfect Union," not a perfect one. To promote and protect the nation, the Constitution commits three categories of power to three separate branches of our federal government. Article I assigns "All legislative powers herein granted" to Congress. Article II places "The executive Power" in the president. And Article III vests the "judicial power of the United States…in one supreme Court, and in such inferior Courts as the Congress may from time to time ordain and establish." The three branches, however, are not completely distinct. For instance, the president may veto acts of Congress, and some of the president's appointments are not effective unless confirmed by the Senate. Moreover, there are many questions concerning interactions between various actors that the constitutional text does not clearly answer.

Perhaps because an incomplete separation of powers is a fundamental part of the constitutional scheme, some of the most important controversies that have arisen in our history have involved disputes about the scope of the powers granted to the president by the general language in Article II. I first read two of those cases — *Myers* v. *United States* (1926) and *Humphrey's Executor* v. *United States* (1935) — as a student in Professor Nathanson's constitutional law class.

The *Myers* opinion is especially memorable, partly because of its length and its detailed discussion of history, and partly because its author was William Howard Taft, who, as mentioned earlier, had served as the chief executive of the United States before becoming the tenth chief justice of the United States. The case held that the "executive Power" vested in the president by Article II of the Constitution included the power to remove a postmaster of the first class — a federal officer whose appointment by the president required Senate confirmation — even though an act of Congress required the president to obtain the consent of the Senate before doing so. Three justices, including Justice Holmes and our professor's former boss Justice Brandeis, dissented. They argued that because Congress had created the office of postmaster, it could also provide job protection for those who filled the office.

In class, we expected our professor to espouse the views of the dissenters, but he never told us how he felt the case should have been decided. Instead, he turned to the facts of *Humphrey's Executor*. There, President Franklin D. Roosevelt had removed a member of the Federal Trade Commission (FTC) whom his immediate predecessor, President Herbert Hoover, had appointed.

Roosevelt took this action in defiance of a provision of the FTC act that was intended to limit his power to do so. Our professor stressed that Roosevelt was certainly justified in reading the broad language in Taft's *Myers* opinion as providing him authority to act as he had. The Court's unanimous opinion in *Humphrey's Executor,* however, disavowed much of Taft's reasoning as unnecessary to the decision in the *Myers* case. It emphasized the fact that the FTC act authorized the commissioners to engage in rule-making and to decide contested cases. These "quasi-legislative" and "quasi-judicial" functions, it reasoned, were not comparable to the purely executive duties of a postmaster. Congress, the Court held, had the power to establish agencies that made and enforced their own rules and were not subject to the control of the president. Thus, President Roosevelt did not have an unlimited power of removal enabling him to exercise control over such agencies.

In his second term as chief justice, William Rehnquist had to confront an even more difficult separation-of-powers issue than those of the postmaster and FTC commissioner cases. *Morrison* v. *Olson* (1988) presented the question whether Congress had violated the constitutional principle of separation of powers by legislating the Ethics in Government Act, which authorized the appointment of an independent prosecutor who was not subject to removal by the president. In his opinion for the Court, the chief concluded that the removal provisions in the statute were more analogous to those upheld in *Humphrey's Executor* than to those that *Myers* had refused to uphold and that the statute was therefore valid. In dissent, Justice Scalia argued that the duties of a prosecutor are unquestionably executive in character and that the case was therefore controlled by Chief Justice Taft's opinion in *Myers*. As a result, Scalia reasoned, the statutory bar on presidential removal of the independent prosecutor ran afoul of the Constitution.

A few days before the opinion was announced, we held our annual end-of-term party for the clerks and other Court employees. As Justice White and I shared some of the available nonalcoholic punch, we noted that no one had made an oral announcement of a dissenting opinion during the term. When Justice Scalia joined us, glass of punch in hand, we talked briefly about Justice Harlan's view that there should be at least one such dissent every year. If memory serves me, Nino, who was then our junior justice, stated that he was unaware of the tradition but welcomed our suggestion that he announce his opinion from the bench. His written opinion failed to persuade any justice not to join the chief, but I think his eloquent oral statement — announced immediately after the chief justice's majority opinion on June 29, 1988 — may have helped to convince some members of Congress that even if the statute was constitutional, it would be unwise to reenact it. When the act expired by its own terms in 1992, it took Congress two years to reauthorize it. It lapsed again in 1999, after Kenneth Starr's investigation under the act had led to President Bill Clinton's impeachment, and has not been reauthorized since.

Another separation-of-powers case in which Bill Rehnquist and I agreed has come to be remembered as part of the narrative of events culminating in the Senate proceedings that followed that impeachment. As chief justice, Rehnquist presided in the Senate during those events. I did not attend any of those sessions but was unsurprised that those who did gave Bill uniformly high marks for his characteristically impartial and efficient leadership. After all, a few years earlier Bill Rehnquist had written one of the few books that deal almost exclusively with the subject of impeachment. The book, entitled *Grand Inquests,* may not have been a bestseller, but the author's study of the subject made him uniquely well qualified to fulfill his constitutional role. Based on my conversations with him at the time, I know that he also enjoyed the departure from his normal routine.

Shortly before those proceedings, the Court had been confronted with the question whether either the Constitution or respect for the office of the president required a federal district court to defer the trial of a damages claim against President Clinton until after the end of his term. In a unanimous opinion that Bill assigned to me, we upheld the decisions of the lower courts denying the request for a stay of the trial. Among the arguments that we rejected was a claim that permitting the trial to proceed would violate the doctrine of separation of powers.

While I am not aware of any significant scholarly criticism of the legal analysis in my opinion, numerous commentators have rather enthusiastically suggested that only the village idiot could have authored one statement that I made. In my response to the argument that the burdens of the litigation would impair the president's ability to discharge his official duties, I declared: "If the past is any indicator, it seems unlikely that a deluge of such litigation will ever engulf the Presidency. As for the case at hand, if properly managed by the District Court, it appears to us highly unlikely to occupy any substantial amount of petitioner's time." Clinton later gave deposition testimony that triggered his impeachment, which, in turn, obviously occupied a huge amount of his time. These events, it is argued, proved my comments to have been ludicrous.

That appraisal depends on a failure to recognize both the difference between a trial and a pretrial deposition and the difference between the trial proceedings and the unforeseen impeachment. A postponement of the trial would not necessarily have justified a postponement of the president's deposition. Indeed, as the president's lawyers stated at oral argument, a delay in the trial would have increased the need for depositions because of the risk that key witnesses' memories might fade. Given that the case (*Clinton v. Jones* [1997]) was settled, we will never know just how much time a trial would have consumed. We do know that our ruling did not give rise to the predicted avalanche of litigation. And the impeachment proceedings were certainly not a part of "the case at hand" referred to in our opinion.

Still, the reaction to my words illustrates that an author is seldom the best judge of how readers will react to his work. I have never written anything that approaches the eloquence of the Gettysburg Address, but I do understand how its author could be so profoundly wrong when he predicted that the "world will little note, nor long remember" his words.

Despite my respect for Bill Rehnquist's efficiency as chief, I hope that some of his opinions for the Court will one day be well described by Lincoln's modest phrase. His death-penalty jurisprudence, for example, is consistent with his frank admiration of Judge Isaac Parker. Parker served as the district judge for the Western District of Arkansas from 1875 until 1896 and became known as the hanging judge because he sentenced 160 defendants to death. Bill quoted from a biography of Parker in an unusual opinion dissenting from the Court's denial of certiorari in a Georgia capital case.

That case featured a defendant who, on direct appeal and in a state postconviction proceeding, argued that pre-trial publicity had created an atmosphere that made it impossible for him to have a fair trial. Justices Brennan and Marshall voted to hear the case because they thought the claim had merit. Bill joined them in seeking to hear the petition, but for a quite different reason: he wanted to establish a special procedure that would conclude capital cases as promptly as possible. He therefore argued that the Court should take the case and decide the federal questions even before the federal district court or the federal court of appeals had an opportunity to do so. His position, if adopted by the Court, would have multiplied the number of capital cases heard on the merits each term.

Bill's remarkably consistent pattern of voting to uphold death sentences coupled with his opinion in *Payne* v. *Tennessee* provide a fair reflection of his contribution to this area of the law. *Payne* was published on June 27, 1991, the last day of the October 1990 term and the day when Thurgood Marshall announced his retirement. In *Payne*, the Court held that the prosecution could produce "victim impact evidence" to support its request for the death penalty. In earlier cases, our jurisprudence had required that any decision to impose the death penalty be based solely on evidence informing the jury about the character of the offense or the character of the defendant. Evidence that serves no purpose other than to appeal to the sympathies and emotions of the jury had never been considered admissible. Indeed, in two cases decided only a few years earlier — before Justices Brennan and Powell retired — we had squarely held that the admission of victim impact evidence was impermissible. I vividly remember Justice Marshall's outraged reaction to the majority's decision to overrule those recent cases. He, of course, had been a great trial lawyer (as had Lewis Powell, who authored one of the two overruled opinions) and so was particularly well qualified to evaluate the significance of such evidentiary rulings. My reaction to that abysmal *Payne* decision remains every bit as hostile today as Thurgood's was when it was announced.

Thurgood's retirement may well have been the most significant judicial event of Bill Rehnquist's tenure as chief justice. When I reflect on its importance, I think first about my memories of his contributions to our conferences and his personal friendship, and second about the changes in the Court's jurisprudence that are attributable to his successor, Clarence Thomas.

Thurgood had, of course, earned national fame and admiration for his work as an appellate lawyer. He had presented the oral argument and been in charge of the briefing in *Brown* v. *Board of Education* and had served as solicitor general of the United States; his appellate expertise was unmatched. In our conferences, however, it was his experience as a trial lawyer in hostile southern communities — buttressed by his son John's more recent experiences as a Virginia state police officer — that most frequently provided the source of his perceptive and original contributions to our debates. Moreover, he had a seemingly inexhaustible inventory of jokes and humorous anecdotes that he shared with us. Most notably, and I am still amazed by this fact, he never told us the same story twice.

As a celebration of Thurgood's eightieth birthday, Bill and Lovida Coleman hosted a dinner in his honor at their home in McLean, Virginia. I assumed that Maryan and I had been invited to that dinner because my friendship with Bill dated back so many years — he had served as a law clerk for Felix Frankfurter the year after I clerked for Wiley Rutledge and had gone on to a distinguished legal career that included serving as secretary of transportation under President Gerald Ford. I learned later, however, that the dinner had been planned by several of the lawyers who had played an important role in the fight to end segregation in the South and that Thurgood was the sole arbiter of the guest list. That bit of after-acquired information made Maryan and me especially proud of our attendance at a memorable and enjoyable social event.

The importance of the change in the Court's jurisprudence that is directly attributable to the choice of Clarence Thomas to fill the vacancy created by Thurgood's retirement cannot be overstated. I discuss one example of Clarence's impact — his writings on the Eighth Amendment — toward the end of this book. More generally, decisions made by five-to-four votes in which Clarence was a member of the majority are evidence of that importance because I am convinced that Thurgood would have voted with the four dissenters in most, if not all, of them. While Thurgood's jurisprudence reflected an understanding that the Constitution was drafted "to form a more perfect Union" — and thus to accommodate unforeseen changes in society — Justice Thomas's repeated emphasis on historical analysis seems to assume that we should view the Union as perfect at the beginning and subject to improvement only by following the cumbersome process of amending the Constitution. Three five-to-four decisions in which Clarence provided the critical vote to invalidate federal gun control laws illustrate the point.

In the first of those cases — *United States* v. *Lopez* (1995) — the majority held that the Gun-Free School Zones Act of 1990, which prohibited the knowing possession of firearms in school zones, exceeded the authority of Congress to regulate interstate commerce. Justice Thomas wrote a separate opinion in which he argued that much of the Court's recent commerce clause jurisprudence was not faithful to the original intent of the framers. I am quite sure that Thurgood would have joined one or more of the dissenting opinions expressing the view that even if the interest in eliminating the market for possession of handguns by schoolchildren would not have justified federal legislation in 1789, it surely does today.

This case has particular meaning for me because it touched upon my work as a clerk for Justice Rutledge. It was Justice Rutledge's practice to write the first drafts of his opinions in longhand, but he allowed each of his clerks to prepare the first draft of one opinion for the Court. My assignment was to draft the opinion in a case called *Mandeville Island Farms, Inc.* v. *American Crystal Sugar Co.* (1948). The question in the case was whether an agreement among California sugar refiners to fix the prices that they paid to California farmers for locally grown sugar beets violated the Sherman Act.

The draft that I gave to the justice succinctly stated that the per se rule against price fixing applied to buyers as well as sellers. As I remember the draft, it was about three or four typewritten pages. (A few sentences from that draft appear on pages 235 and 236 of an opinion in volume 334 of the U.S. Reports that is twenty-six pages long.) Justice Rutledge decided that it would be appropriate to explain why the Court's miserly interpretation of the Sherman Act and the commerce clause in *United States* v. *E. C. Knight Co.* — a case decided in 1895 — was no longer good law.

In writing my draft, I assumed that there was no need to restate the basic propositions of doctrine that my classmates and I had been taught in law school. The distinction between manufacture and commerce on which the *E. C. Knight* Court had relied in defining the scope of Congress's power under the commerce clause had been a relic of the past after the Court's adoption of the rule of reason in the *Standard Oil* case in 1911 and its decision in the *Shreveport Rate Cases* in 1914. Justice Rutledge's opinion cogently explained why.

In the years following my clerkship, and indeed during the first nineteen years of my tenure on the Court, I continued to regard Justice Rutledge's revision of my first draft as an unnecessary, though lucid and accurate, piece of scholarly writing on a topic that he had thoroughly mastered. In *Lopez,* however, Clarence provided me with evidence that Justice Rutledge's thorough repudiation of the reasoning in the *E. C. Knight* case had been entirely appropriate. For in his concurring opinion in *Lopez,* Thomas unequivocally endorsed the reasoning in the *E. C. Knight* case. It is quite clear that were it up to him, Justice Thomas would not merely rewrite the only Court opinion that I had an opportunity to draft as a clerk but would overrule the case itself.

The second case involving guns in which Clarence's vote was decisive was *Printz* v. *United States* (1997). There, history, rather than constitutional text, provided the critical role in the majority's decision to invalidate the provision in the Brady Handgun Violence Prevention Act that required local law enforcement officers to make background checks of prospective handgun purchasers during the period before a national system could be implemented. There was no doubt that the commerce clause provided ample authority for the federal statute, but the majority held that the provision violated a rule that they had previously announced prohibiting Congress from requiring state officers to perform federal duties. Two dissenting opinions — including my own — explained why the majority's historical analysis was incorrect; I added this comment about why it was also profoundly unwise:

> Indeed, since the ultimate issue is one of power, we must consider its implications in times of national emergency. Matters such as the enlistment of air raid wardens, the administration of a military draft, the mass inoculation of children to forestall an epidemic, or perhaps the threat of an international terrorist, may require a national response before federal personnel can be made available to respond.

I often wonder whether the tragic events of 9/11 have given members of the majority any second thoughts about the wisdom of their decision. I find it hard to believe that they would adhere to their flawed historical analysis today.

The third case, in which debatable historic analysis again

played a more important role than constitutional text, is *District of Columbia* v. *Heller* (2008). In that case a bare majority of the Court held that the Second Amendment protects the right of an individual to keep a handgun at home. In 1939, in the *Miller* case, a unanimous Court had held that the scope of the right protected by the amendment was delimited by its relationship to the preservation of a well-regulated militia. That holding was directly supported by the text of the amendment's preamble stating that a well-regulated militia is necessary for the security of a free state.

My firm conviction that Thurgood's vote would have led to a different result in that case is supported by my recollection of his views on the matter and by his respect for the doctrine of stare decisis set forth in his dissenting opinion in *Payne*. Thurgood's commendable faith in and respect for the decisions of his predecessors was not always evident in the decisions of his colleagues.

One cannot underestimate the importance of changes caused by Court opinions authored by Rehnquist in a quite different area of the law: that governing the duty of the states to comply with federal law. That duty is defined in Article VI of the Constitution, which contains this paragraph:

> This Constitution, and the Laws of the United States which shall be made in Pursuance thereof; and all Treaties made or which shall be made, under the Authority of the United States, shall be the supreme Law of the Land; and the Judges in every State shall be bound thereby, any Thing in the Constitution or Laws of any State to the Contrary notwithstanding.

That duty had been succinctly and correctly described in 1936, when the Court rejected the State of California's claim that its status as a sovereign state limited the power of Congress to regulate its commercial activities. As Chief Justice Harlan Stone wrote for a unanimous Court that included Justices Louis Brandeis and Benjamin Cardozo, "there is no such limitation upon the plenary power to regulate commerce. The state can no more deny the power if its exercise has been authorized by Congress than can an individual" (*United States* v. *California*).

Forty years later, in his opinion for the five-justice majority in *National League of Cities* v. *Usery* (1976), then Justice Rehnquist confidently asserted that that statement was "simply wrong." He thought it clear that when a state acts as a state in the conduct of governmental functions — in that case, by deciding how much to pay its employees — the federal power is not supreme. I was one of the four dissenters, and I later joined the opinion in *Garcia* v. *San Antonio Metropolitan Transit Authority* (1985) that overruled *National League of Cities*. It is now settled that the federal power over the labor market includes the power to prevent states from paying their employees substandard wages and discriminating against them for impermissible reasons. States, just like counties, cities, and individual citizens, have a duty to obey federal law. It thus was Justice Rehnquist, rather than Justice Stone, who was "simply wrong" in his evaluation of the state's immunity from federal regulation under the commerce clause.

But the Rehnquist understanding of the importance of state sovereign immunity retains its vitality in cases brought against states by private citizens alleging violations of their federal rights. It was his opinion in 1974 in *Edelman* v. *Jordan* — a case in which Illinois had failed to make payments that were required by the federal Social Security Act — that breathed new life into the Eleventh Amendment. As I have noted, that amendment was adopted in 1795 in response to the Supreme Court's holding that a federal court had jurisdiction over a suit brought against the State of Georgia by two citizens of South Carolina (who happened to be executors of a British creditor). Neither the opinions in that case nor the text of the Eleventh Amendment, which merely protects states from suits brought by nonresident plaintiffs, had anything to say about suits brought to enforce federal rights.

Before Justice Rehnquist wrote his *Edelman* opinion, most lawyers and federal judges assumed that the Court's decision in *Ex parte Young* (1908) had eliminated the Eleventh Amendment as a possible defense to suits against states and state officials to enforce federal rights. Likely as a result, the Illinois officers who were the defendants in *Edelman* did not initially assert that the Eleventh Amendment barred the proceeding against them; indeed, they never even made that argument before the district court. Shortly before the Supreme Court heard arguments in *Edelman,* the Court summarily affirmed judgments against state officials in three similar cases. Nonetheless, while acknowledging that under *Ex parte Young* the Eleventh Amendment did not bar prospective relief, and despite having no textual basis for its action, the five-justice *Edelman* majority held that the amendment did bar any judicial order requiring the state to pay to the plaintiffs the amount of welfare benefits that had been wrongfully withheld from them. In the ensuing years, Rehnquist transformed his *Edelman* opinion into a font of authority with which to effect a sea change in the Court's sovereign immunity doctrine. He thus relied on judicial interpretations rather than anything in the text of the Eleventh Amendment as authority for a series of opinions for five-justice majorities that invalidated numerous acts of Congress. During his tenure the Court invalidated forty-one federal statutes — an unprecedented number and almost three times as many as the fourteen under the Hughes Court that prompted President Roosevelt's unsuccessful Court-packing plan in 1933.

Rehnquist's opinion in *Seminole Tribe of Fla.* v. *Florida* (1996) is unquestionably the most important opinion in this line of cases and the most important of any sort that he authored as chief justice of the United States. There, relying on sovereign immunity and prior misinterpretations of the Eleventh Amendment, the Court invalidated the provision in the Indian Gaming Regulatory Act that authorized the Seminole Tribe to sue the State of Florida to enforce its statutory rights.

Because the chief's opinion and the dissents occupy nearly 140 pages of the official reports, I cannot begin to summarize all of the debate or even the explanation advanced for overruling a seven-year-old decision in which the Court had upheld the enforceability of a federal remedy against Pennsylvania for environmental damages that the state had caused. In essence, the majority in *Seminole Tribe* converted the common-law doctrine of sovereign immunity into a constitutional rule. This matters because Congress can modify common-law rules, but its legislation does not amend the Constitution.

The extraordinary consequences of the holding were to preclude Congress from authorizing private plaintiffs to recover damages for a state's violation of federal law. Whereas the Eleventh Amendment itself dealt only with the jurisdiction of the federal courts in suits brought against states by noncitizens, the logical implication of *Seminole Tribe*—at least according to the five-justice majority in *Alden* v. *Maine* (1999) — is preclusion of private litigation to enforce federal rights in both state and federal courts.

Rather than my repeating the dissenters' explanation of the errors in the majority's reliance on history rather than legal text, it seems appropriate to make just three brief comments on the interest in protecting the "dignity" of the sovereign states. As the text of Article VI that I have quoted makes perfectly clear, the State of New York and the City of New York have precisely the same duty to obey federal law. The fact that a former colony was an independent "sovereign" during the few years between the Declaration of Independence and the ratification of the Constitution does not provide a rational basis for granting New York's state government an immunity that is not available to New York City.

The common-law doctrine of sovereign immunity originated in England and was the product of a belief that the king could do no wrong, and even if he did sin, only God could decide the appropriate remedy. As Thomas Macaulay explained in his classic history of England, that conception of sovereignty was rejected in 1688 when the abysmal reign of James II came to an end:

> Unhappily the Church had long taught the nation that hereditary monarchy, alone among our institutions, was divine and inviolable; that the right of the House of Commons to share in the legislative power was a right merely human, but that the right of the king to the obedience of

his people was from above; that the Great Charter was a statute which might be repealed by those who had made it, but that the rule which called the princes of the blood royal to the throne in order of succession was of celestial origin, and that any Act of Parliament inconsistent with that rule was a nullity. It is evident that, in a society in which such superstitions prevail, constitutional freedom must ever be insecure. A power which is regarded merely as the ordinance of man cannot be an efficient check on a power which is regarded as the ordinance of God. It is vain to hope that laws however excellent, will permanently restrain a king who in his own opinion, and in that of a great part of his people, has an authority infinitely higher in kind than the authority which belongs to those laws. To deprive royalty of these mysterious attributes, and to establish the principle that kings reigned by a right in no respect differing from the right by which freeholders chose knights of the shire, or from the right by which judges granted writs of Habeas Corpus, was absolutely necessary to the security of our liberties.

Depriving a state of the mysterious right to protect its dignity from its own citizens is equally necessary to protect the federal rights of those citizens.

Justice James Wilson, who played a leading role in the drafting of our Constitution, made the point better than I can. Before the Eleventh Amendment was adopted, he made this comment on sovereignty on this side of the Atlantic:

To the Constitution of the *United States* the term SOVEREIGN, is totally unknown. There is but one place where it could have been used with propriety. But, even in that place it would not, perhaps, have comported with the delicacy of those, who *ordained* and *established* that Constitution. They *might* have announced themselves "SOVEREIGN" people of the *United States*: But serenely conscious of the *fact*, they avoided the *ostentatious declaration*.

Like the gold stripes on his robes, Chief Justice Rehnquist's writing about sovereignty was ostentatious and more reflective of the ancient British monarchy than our modern republic. I am hopeful that his writings in this area will not be long remembered.

As in both earlier and later years, on Friday, December 8, 2000, Maryan and I took our granddaughters, Hannah and Haley, and their parents to the annual Christmas party at the National Gallery of Art on Constitution Avenue. It is always an especially enjoyable occasion that gives youngsters an opportunity to converse with a juggler, a clown, a magician, and a man on stilts and to engage in treasure hunts and coloring exercises while learning something about great works of art.

Earlier that day, the Florida Supreme Court had issued an opinion ordering state election officials to spend the weekend conducting a manual recount of votes cast in that state in the presidential election. On the basis mostly of voting machine tallies, George Bush led Al Gore by a statewide margin of 537 votes.

Chief Justice Roberts and family and Justice Stevens and family at the National Gallery of Art Christmas party on December 8, 2006.

Pictured in front row: Josephine Roberts, Jack Roberts, Maryan Stevens, Justice Stevens, Haley Mullen, and Kevin Mullen. Pictured in second row: Jane Roberts, Chief Justice Roberts, Hannah Mullen, and Sue Mullen.

Based largely on the fact that in Miami-Dade County about nine thousand ballots registered as nonvotes by the machines had never been manually reviewed, the Florida court had decided that state law required a recount. Promptly responding to that decision, counsel for Bush filed an application in the United States Supreme Court asking us to halt the recount by entering a stay. When I bumped into Justice Stephen Breyer at the Christmas party, we had a brief conversation about the stay application. We agreed that the application was frivolous. To secure a stay, a litigant must show that one is necessary to prevent a legally cognizable irreparable injury. Bush's attorneys had failed to make any such showing.

I found the case particularly easy because I had been confronted with a similar issue as a member of a three-judge district court shortly after becoming a court of appeals judge in 1970. In *Roudebush* v. *Hartke* (1971), I had dissented from an order prohibiting state election officials from conducting a recount of the votes cast in the race for the office of U.S. senator from Indiana. I wrote that the plaintiff had "failed to prove that he would suffer irreparable harm if the recount were permitted to proceed." Observing that the United States Senate would make the final determination as to which candidate to seat, I explained that the Senate's decision likely "would be facilitated, rather than impaired, by the availability of a fairly conducted recount." The Supreme Court agreed, noting that Indiana had determined that recounts were sometimes "necessary to guard against irregularity and error in the tabulation of votes." There was "no reason to suppose that a court-appointed recount commission would be less honest or conscientious in the performance of its duties than the precinct election boards that initially counted the ballots," and it concluded that it "would be no more than speculation to assume that the Indiana recount procedure would impair...an independent evaluation by the Senate."

Because the Constitution also lays out procedures under which Congress determines which presidential candidate has won, the history of *Roudebush* made it particularly easy for me to conclude that we should allow the Florida recount to proceed. Justice Breyer expressed the same opinion, and we went our separate ways confidently assuming that the stay application would be denied when we met the next day.

On Saturday, the Court — by a vote of five to four — granted the stay, ordered the parties to file written briefs on Sunday, and set the case for argument on Monday. After the argument we held a brief conference, and on Tuesday we issued six opinions. To the best of my knowledge no justice has ever cited any of them. What I still regard as a frivolous stay application kept the Court extremely busy for four days.

VII

John Roberts Jr.

John G. Roberts Jr., Chief Justice (2005–)

As children in Michigan City, Indiana, well over a century ago, my mother and the daughter of the warden of the Indiana state prison were neighbors and playmates. My mother later taught English in high school in Michigan City; after she and my father married, in 1907, they built a summer home in Lakeside, Michigan, a few miles away. When I was in grammar school and, later, high school, our family spent our summers in Lakeside, and in 1961, I built my own summer home there. I took flying lessons at the nearby Oselka Airport, a few miles from Three Oaks, Michigan. I have always loved that part of the Midwest.

In 1969, John Roberts was a high school freshman in a boarding school in La Porte, Indiana, a few minutes away from Oselka Airport. His home was in nearby Long Beach, Indiana, just north of Michigan City, and his father commuted to work at the Bethlehem steel mill in Burns Harbor, Indiana, passing by Michigan City and the venerable prison that is still operating today. At that time, I kept my plane at Oselka and often landed at the small airports in La Porte and Michigan City. It is possible, I suppose, that John saw my plane in flight during those years or that I saw him or his home from the air. But even though it is unlikely that our paths actually crossed then, our shared knowledge about that part of the Midwest helped us form a solid friendship when we became colleagues in Washington, D.C., many years later.

John's future differed dramatically from the future of Oselka

Airport. Years later, while considering a Supreme Court case involving the constitutionality of state laws regulating the interstate transportation of garbage, I was shocked to learn that the Oselka landing strip where I had done touch-and-goes when I was learning to fly was gone. It had become a garbage dump.

John's subsequent years, by contrast, were marked by a series of stunning accomplishments. After ranking first in his high school class, he graduated from Harvard College summa cum laude in 1976. In each of the three summers when he was a student at Harvard, he worked as an assistant electrician in the Bethlehem steel mill in Burns Harbor, Indiana. He was frequently shocked on the job — not by startling, newfound knowledge but rather by electrical discharges that arose when he connected or disconnected terminals. His summer earnings helped to pay for his college education. In 1979 he graduated from Harvard Law School magna cum laude. A year later, Henry Friendly, one of our greatest federal judges, hired him as a law clerk. Then Justice Rehnquist selected the man who would ultimately succeed him as chief justice of the United States to be his law clerk.

I am sure that it was John's legal acumen rather than his skills as a tennis player that motivated Bill Rehnquist's decision to hire him. I have reached this conclusion for two reasons. First, one of Roberts's co-clerks, Dean Colson, had competed at Wimbledon and was obviously the clerk best qualified to serve as the justice's partner during the Rehnquist chambers' weekly doubles games. (My own recollection reinforces this conclusion. I played against Colson in a doubles game one weekend. His first serves were invisible bullets and even his second serves had topspins that produced gigantic bounces and made them unreturnable for me.)

Second, although John was a successful high school athlete, tennis was not his best sport. He was captain of the football team, playing in the backfield on both offense and defense. Like my friend Byron White, who was an All-American at Colorado, John played sixty-minute games and was a member of both the offensive and defensive squads. (Having had a law partner — Jack Barry — who also played sixty minutes of the game, in his case for an undefeated Notre Dame team, I have always been impressed by that statistic whenever I watch the modern version of the sport.) Roberts was also a member of the wrestling team and had won all but two of his matches in the 126-pound class. In order for John to compete he had to beat a teammate of the same size in a practice match; the loser of the practice match had to compete against larger and presumably stronger opponents. John won those practice matches on a fairly regular basis. (Whether it was owing to a coincidence or John's access to a scouting report, he lost the practice match when the 126-pound opponent he would have competed against next happened to be the state champion at that weight.)

John's interest in football included occasional attendance at Notre Dame games in South Bend. Despite his respect for that team and that school, however, he did not always root for the home team. His father was a graduate of the University of Pittsburgh, and family loyalty took precedence over local enthusiasm when Pitt was the visiting team.

Following his clerkship, John Roberts had careers in both the executive branch of the federal government and in private practice that eminently qualified him to be a Supreme Court justice.

His public service included stints as a special assistant to the attorney general, associate counsel to the president, principal deputy solicitor general, and a judge on the United States Court of Appeals for the D.C. Circuit. His private practice was equally successful and included a partnership at the firm of Hogan and Hartson and the completion of thirty-nine oral arguments in our Court before joining our bench. Although that figure is impressive — it exceeds, I believe, the numbers for such great advocates as Thurgood Marshall and Ruth Ginsburg — it is only a fraction of the arguments made by Daniel Webster, John W. Davis, Erwin Griswold, and a lawyer from Virginia named Walter Jones, who made scores and scores of arguments during the antebellum period.

But far more important than the quantity of John Roberts's arguments was the quality. He was not only articulate and persuasive but also totally honest in his descriptions of the facts and the relevant legal precedents in every case. Having heard all of those arguments, I consider myself well qualified to testify that he was a superb lawyer.

In my judgment, both at the time the decisions were made and now, he was the obvious first choice to fill any vacancy that might occur on the Court while George W. Bush was president. Thus, I welcomed the decision to select him to succeed Justice O'Connor when she announced her retirement and the subsequent decision to make him the chief justice when Bill Rehnquist died.

After the Senate confirmed John Roberts's appointment as chief justice, it became my duty to administer the oath of office in a ceremony at the White House. I was then the senior justice on the Court and had been acting as its chief justice since Bill Rehnquist's death. Performing that duty presented me with a problem because I believe that the ceremony should take place at the Supreme Court whenever possible. The three branches of our government are separate and equal. The president and the Senate play critical roles in the nomination and confirmation process. After that process ends, however, the "separate but equal" regime takes over. (Chief Justice Rehnquist, as I have mentioned, properly treated Senator Specter like any other litigant.)

When I was sworn in as a justice, President Ford came to the Court and, as a member of our bar, participated in the ceremony. In 1981, when Sandra Day O'Connor was sworn in, President Reagan came to the Court and witnessed the administration of her oath. When Chief Justice Rehnquist and Justice Scalia were sworn in, however, the ceremony was held in the White House. And when Reagan's next appointee, Anthony Kennedy, was sworn in, not only was the ceremony conducted at the White House but the president participated with remarks that welcomed his new appointee as a judge who would follow the law rather than make it up. I thought the president's remarks were both offensive and inappropriate and therefore decided not to attend similar ceremonies at the White House in the future.

The first President Bush and President Clinton followed the Reagan precedent. Justices David Souter, Clarence Thomas, Ruth Ginsburg, and Stephen Breyer were all sworn in at the White House. I did not attend any of those ceremonies. In each case, I explained to my new colleague the reason for my absence, assuring each that it was not motivated by any regret about his or her addition to our team. I was tempted to adhere to that lonely position when asked to come to the White House to administer the oath to John Roberts but concluded that a refusal to participate would have been widely misinterpreted as manifesting disapproval of his appointment.

Subsequent events have convinced me that I made the right decision. My refusals to attend White House ceremonies may have affected President Obama's decision to attend the investitures of Justice Sonia Sotomayor and Justice Elena Kagan at the Court. And, despite my misgiving, I like to think that my participation in the Roberts ceremony reflected and supported the view that our common interest in administering justice impartially is far more important than any individual's interest in advancing his or her own point of view. I think Chief Justice Roberts's decision to attend President Obama's State of the Union address in 2011 despite the debate that had ensued after the president's criticism of the Court's decision in the *Citizens United* campaign financing case in his address a year earlier also reflected and supported that view. Moreover, the first decision that he made in his capacity as chief justice of the United States was unquestionably correct and consistent with his role as the first among equals: he decided not to decorate his robes with gold stripes.

In John Roberts's first term as chief justice, 8,521 cases were filed in the Supreme Court. That is almost exactly twice the number filed in Bill Rehnquist's first term as chief justice: 4,240. More striking than that statistic, however, is the fact that there were only about half as many oral arguments in Roberts's initial term as in Rehnquist's — 90 for Roberts and 175 for Rehnquist. What had been a docket that required each of us to write about twenty majority opinions in each term during the Rehnquist years was essentially cut in half. While I had been the justice who most frequently voted to deny petitions for certiorari when Warren Burger was chief justice, I think I was the one who most frequently voted to grant in cases that were denied while I was still on the Court during the Roberts regime.

Although I cannot confidently explain the reasons for that dramatic reduction of the number of oral arguments, I can identify three possible causes. First, of course, is the repeal of much of the Court's mandatory jurisdiction in 1988; before that date, in each term the Court would probably have disposed of as many as ten unmeritorious appeals without argument if it had had the discretion to do so. Second, in my judgment the number of cases in which the courts of appeals have reached conflicting conclusions is smaller than it once was; more significant, increasingly careful analysis of cert petitions has frequently persuaded the Court that what at first blush appears to be an important conflict is in fact either not a conflict at all or insignificant. Third, I believe that the use of a cert pool in which one law clerk prepares a single memo for most of the justices creates a subtle bias against granting review in close cases. A recommendation to deny is less likely to produce an unfavorable reaction from any of the justices than a recommendation to grant and is therefore attractive to a risk-averse clerk. And even though the justices decide for themselves whether to grant, a busy judge's first impression of a case is sometimes sufficient to control his or her final vote.

Whatever the explanation may be, it is now clear that the

arguments favoring the creation of an intermediate court of appeals — the primary one being that it would ease the burden on the Supreme Court — that were debated at some length when Warren Burger was the chief are totally unpersuasive today.

With regard to all of his special responsibilities, John Roberts is an excellent chief justice. Perhaps he is not quite as efficient as his predecessor when presiding in open court or in the Court's conferences, but his occasional and minor deviations from strict enforcement are well justified. His own extensive experience as an advocate may have made him slightly more generous in allowing a few comments after the red light is turned on, but in my judgment those allowances have always been appropriate.

In our private conferences he was always a well-prepared, fair, and effective leader. For instance, when I added cases to the list of cert petitions to be discussed — that is, when I asked that the conference discuss petitions for certiorari that the chief had not thought worth our attention — it was apparent that he always took a second look at them. By the time the conference arrived, he was prepared to explain his vote to deny, or to acknowledge that there were valid reasons for considering a grant. He also welcomed more discussion of the merits of the argued cases than his predecessor — including expansions of the reasoning behind his own votes — but he maintained the appropriate impartiality in giving each of us an opportunity to speak. In sum, he is a better presiding officer than both of his immediate predecessors.

With the possible exception of Earl Warren, he is also the best spokesman for the Court in nonjudicial functions. He handles meetings with foreign dignitaries with grace, good humor, and understanding of our common problems. His appointments of Jim Duff as head of the administrative office of the judicial branch and Jeff Minear as counselor to the chief justice were both superb. Jim was the aide at the Court in the cloaking room when I first started, and Jeff had been an excellent advocate in the solicitor general's office before the chief persuaded him to come to the Court, where he makes sure that the chief's administrative responsibilities are competently performed. And John Roberts retained our superbly competent clerk, General Bill Suter, and our excellent marshal, Pam Talkin, who had been selected by his predecessor. In sum, I have nothing but praise for his conduct of the responsibilities for which he receives additional compensation.

When I arrived at the Court in 1975, the space occupied by active and retired justices had expanded to include the entire perimeter of the first floor. The chief's chambers had not moved, but instead of five sets of offices on his end of the building, there were only three — the chief's, Potter Stewart's, and Thurgood Marshall's. Each of the three other members of the Court appointed by President Nixon — Harry Blackmun, Lewis Powell, and Bill Rehnquist — had chambers with a glorious view of the Capitol to the west. Justice Douglas, whom I succeeded, wanted to retain his chambers, and retired justice Tom Clark had offices to the east of Bill Rehnquist's. I moved into the only available vacant space on the first floor — the suite that was traditionally reserved for the retired chief justice. Given that both Stone and Vinson had died in office, I believe that what was probably the most beautiful office in the Court had been vacant for about thirty years. It has the inspiring view of the Capitol but inadequate accommodations for multiple law clerks.

The office was particularly impressive in 1975 because it contained two magnificent crystal chandeliers. Those chandeliers played a role in what I regard as an unfortunate change in the conference room that occurred during John Roberts's tenure as chief. A few years ago, Justice O'Connor, Justice Kennedy, and Justice Souter served as a committee supervising much-needed renovations of the Supreme Court Building, including such matters as modernizing its antiquated heating system. As a part of their project they decided to improve the lighting and the appearance of the Court's conference room by removing the two chandeliers from the retired chief's chambers, acquiring a third, and hanging all three in the conference room.

During the summer a year or so before David retired — when the Court was in recess — they made a change in the arrangement of the furniture in the conference room without consulting all of the other justices first. Some might consider the change trivial, but I thought that moving the large oblong table around which the nine justices sit during their conferences could end up having a subtle and unfortunate impact on deliberations. Whereas previously the table had been next to the fireplace at the north end of the room, with the chief sitting at its east end, now the table is aligned on a north–south axis in the center of the room immediately under the new chandelier; the chief sits at the south end of the table, and the senior associate justice sits at the opposite end.

On more than one occasion I voiced an objection to the

change. I think a combination of inertia and gratitude for the countless hours that the three members of the committee had spent, rather than an evaluation of the merits of their decision, led to the consensus accepting the new arrangement.

What formerly was an empty spacious area in the center of the room is now occupied by the table, the nine justices' chairs, and, when the conference is in session, their mobile carts containing all the briefs they need to consult during deliberations. I think the elimination of the large open space in the middle of the room will have an adverse impact on activities on both sides and both ends of the table. At almost every conference at least one justice will have his messenger place one or more photographs of the entire Court on a table behind the chief, implicitly asking for everyone to autograph them. There used to be ample room for multiple justices to do so simultaneously while carrying on a conversation. Seriatim signings are now more common.

When the table was at the north end of the room, the telephone was within arm's reach of the justice sitting to the left of the senior associate justice. The phone is typically used only for outgoing calls, because incoming messages — or materials requested by a justice — are always preceded by a knock on the door from an attendant outside the conference room. On rare occasions when the phone did ring it was safe to assume that the caller had the wrong number. (Byron White typically answered by picking up the phone and crisply stating: "Joe's Bar.") Now the justices must either let the phone ring or get up and cross the room to answer it.

When the conference recesses for the all-important coffee break, a member of the chief's staff brings in the beverages and food and places them on a table on the east side of the room, and the standing justices help themselves to tea and coffee and small plates of fruit or baked goods. There used to be ample room for milling about while discussing nonlegal subjects, such as the Redskins' prospects in the upcoming Sunday game. The congested area between the two tables is now far less accommodating.

The foregoing attempt to explain my reasons for disapproving of the location of the conference table under the central chandelier has provided me with the same benefit that writing first drafts of opinions occasionally did. I have failed to recognize the significance of a critically important fact: sitting in the middle of the room, I seemed to have more difficulty hearing everything that the chief and Ruth Ginsburg had to say. While I had attributed that difficulty to the decline in my hearing capacity, I am now inclined to believe that the acoustics in the middle of the room may differ from those in the area where the table was formerly located. If that should be the case, I shall expect my good friend Nino Scalia, who now sits at the north end of the table, to join this dissent in due course.

Chief Justice Roberts's opinion announcing the judgment of the Court in *Baze* v. *Rees,* in 2008, had a critical impact on my views about the constitutionality of capital punishment. To explain why, I must go back a few years.

In the *Furman* case in 1972, in a one-paragraph unsigned opinion, the Court held that the imposition and carrying out of the death penalty in a series of cases that had arisen in Texas and Georgia constituted cruel and unusual punishment in violation of the Eighth and Fourteenth Amendments. That brief per curiam statement was followed by 231 pages of opinions, one opinion for each of the nine members of the Court. Justices Douglas, Brennan, Stewart, White, and Marshall supported the judgment; Chief Justice Burger and Justices Blackmun, Powell, and Rehnquist dissented. Following that decision, thirty-four state legislatures enacted new death penalty statutes, five of which were challenged during my first term on the Court. The chief justice, Justice White, Justice Blackmun, and Justice Rehnquist voted to uphold the constitutionality of all five, whereas Justices Brennan and Marshall would have invalidated all of them. The joint opinions written by Justice Stewart, Justice Powell, and myself therefore controlled the outcome in all five cases.

We concluded that the so-called mandatory statutes that required the judge to impose the death penalty for every defendant found guilty of certain offenses were unconstitutional, whereas those that required a separate weighing of aggravating and mitigating factors in each case before the death sentence could be imposed were constitutional. That meant that the Georgia and Florida statutes were valid, and the South Carolina and Louisiana statutes were invalid. The Texas statute presented a closer question, but we ultimately decided that it belonged in the nonmandatory category and upheld its validity.

While I was deliberating about the cases, my law clerk George Rutherglen, who is now a professor at the University of Virginia Law School, urged me to treat the Texas statute as effectively mandatory because the jury was required to impose the death penalty if it made a particular finding about the dangerous character of the defendant. George failed to persuade me at the time, but I have since concluded that he was right and that I should have voted differently in the Texas case. Of course, unless I could have persuaded Lewis and Potter to do so as well, the outcome would not have changed. Nevertheless I regret that vote because experience has shown that the Texas statute has played an important role in authorizing so many death sentences in that state.

During our deliberations, both Lewis — who had dissented in *Furman* — and I were influenced by Potter's opinion in that case. He argued that the death sentences before the Court were "cruel and unusual in the same way that being struck by lightning is cruel and unusual" and that the Constitution could not tolerate the infliction of a sentence of death under legal systems "that permit this unique penalty to be so wantonly and so freakishly imposed." Our decisions in 1976 were thus based on our understanding that the states had narrowed the category of death-eligible offenses and would enforce procedures that would minimize the risk of error and the risk that the race of the defendant or the race of the victim would play a role in the sentencing decision.

In a series of cases decided between 1976 and 2008, when Chief Justice Roberts drafted his opinion in the *Baze* case, the Court (over my dissent) had enlarged the category of death-eligible offenses to include felony murder; authorized jury selection procedures that give prosecutors a better opportunity to impanel conviction-prone juries than in ordinary criminal cases; refused to set aside a Georgia death sentence notwithstanding its assumption that the defendant had established that the race of the victim correlated strongly with decisions whether to impose capital punishment; and overruled decisions — one of which was written by Justice Powell — that prohibited the use of victim impact testimony in capital sentencing proceedings. The net effect of those unfortunate decisions had been to increase the danger that emotion, rather than reason, would have a controlling impact on sentencing decisions in capital cases.

In those years, the increasing use of life sentences without the possibility of parole had, in my judgment, eliminated the interest in preventing the defendant from committing further crimes and from deterring others from doing so as sufficient justifications for capital sentences. Moreover, the finality of the death penalty always includes the risk that the state may put an innocent person to death.

Although it is largely forgotten today, concern with execution of innocents led to Michigan's pathbreaking 1846 decision to abolish capital punishments for all nontreasonous crimes. Shortly before Michigan amended its laws, two innocent men — one in Canada and one in New York — had been executed. Also apparently concerned with the fallibility of capital punishment, Wisconsin and Rhode Island soon followed Michigan's abolition. Execution of innocents, after all, is intolerable. That concern has not disappeared. In the last four decades, more than one hundred death-row inmates have been exonerated, a number of them on the basis of DNA evidence.

To the extent that there is any justification for capital punishment today, it is the interest in retribution, making the defendant suffer as his victim had suffered. Retribution — whether based on real or imagined underlying crimes — was no doubt the primary motivation for the gruesome executions conducted by the English monarchs in the sixteenth and seventeenth centuries, for the scourge of lynchings in the South during the nineteenth and early twentieth centuries, and for sentences now being imposed on our most vicious killers. It is that interest that I believe best explains the survival of the death penalty in the United States after its abolition in most civilized countries.

John Roberts's opinion in *Baze,* to my surprise, convinced me that the Court had already rejected the premise that the death penalty serves a meaningful retributive purpose. His review of our earlier cases effectively demonstrated that the Eighth Amendment has been construed to prohibit needless suffering and significant risks of harm to the defendant. As a matter of constitutional law, what was once a gruesome event has been transformed into a procedure comparable to the administration of anesthesia in a hospital operating room. By requiring that an execution be relatively painless, we protect the inmate from enduring any punishment that is comparable to the suffering inflicted on his victim. We have thus undermined the premise on which public approval of the retribution rationale is based.

Reflection after reading the Roberts opinion led to my decision to concur in his result but also to write separately. Quoting from an earlier opinion by Justice White, I stated that the death penalty represents "the pointless and needless extinction of life with only marginal contributions to any discernible social or public purposes."

John Roberts has written two opinions answering questions of constitutional law that merit special comment: his opinion for the Court in *Snyder* v. *Phelps,* concerning the First Amendment, and his opinion in *Graham* v. *Florida,* involving the Eighth

Amendment. The centerpiece of the former, a case involving speech intended to inflict emotional distress on the family of a deceased Marine during his funeral, was this oft-quoted statement by Justice Brennan:

> If there is a bedrock principle underlying the First Amendment, it is that government may not prohibit the expression of an idea simply because society finds the idea itself offensive or disagreeable.

There is some irony in the chief's reliance on that statement because four years earlier he had written the Court opinion upholding the discipline of a high school student for displaying a cryptic banner that might reasonably have been construed as promoting the use of illegal drugs.

Justice Brennan had made the quoted statement in his opinion holding that a Texas statute prohibiting flag burning was unconstitutional. In that case the defendant had taken a flag removed from a public building, doused it with kerosene, and ignited it as part of a public protest against the policies of the Reagan administration. He was not in fact punished for expressing any ideas about those policies; he was punished because he was using a prohibited method of expressing his message.

Justice Brennan had reasoned that the defendant was expressing his disagreement with not only President Reagan but also the idea that the flag was a symbol that was entitled to respect. But again, it was not the expression of that idea that gave rise to the prohibition; it was the method of expressing the idea that the law prohibited. The law would have allowed the defendant to express his hatred of the flag in many other ways, but it would not have allowed him to shoot or to assault a soldier carrying a flag to express his hatred.

Reasonable scholars and judges have offered differing views about whether flag burning should be a constitutionally protected method of expression, but I am not persuaded that Justice Brennan's eloquent statement helped answer the question in either the flag case or the funeral-hate-speech case. Although seven of his colleagues joined Chief Justice Roberts's opinion that relied on the Brennan proposition, as Justice Alito explained in his dissent, the hate speech during the funeral was not prohibited because society or the jury found the speakers' ideas disagreeable and offensive. It was prohibited because the jury found that the speakers intended to use their speech to cause severe harm to a grieving family during a funeral.

Our cases interpreting the First Amendment have recognized a critical difference between harmful speech targeting public figures and similar speech about private individuals. While some defamatory speech about public figures, like the Reverend Jerry Falwell, is protected, similar speech about private individuals is not. The fact that the protection of such speech may shine a spotlight on the speakers does not, as Justice Alito explained, "transform their statements attacking the character of a private figure into statements that made a contribution to debate on matters of public concern." And though the protest in this case occurred on a public street, Justice Alito elaborated, "there is no reason why a public street in close proximity to the scene of a funeral should be regarded as a free-fire zone in which otherwise actionable verbal attacks are shielded from liability."

It is easy to gloss over the difference between prohibitions against the expression of particular ideas — which fall squarely within the First Amendment's prohibition of rules "abridging the freedom of speech" — and prohibitions of certain methods of expression that allow ample room for using other methods of expressing the same ideas. The difference is much like the difference between speech itself and money that is used to finance speech. Given the fact that most of his colleagues joined the chief in his funeral-speech opinion, perhaps I should give him a passing grade in First Amendment law. But for reasons that it took me ninety pages to explain in my dissent in the *Citizens United* campaign finance case, his decision to join the majority in that case prevents me from doing so.

The chief is, however, entitled to a high grade for his separate writing in *Graham* v. *Florida* (2010), a case in which Justice Anthony Kennedy's majority opinion held that imposing a life sentence without the possibility of parole on a juvenile offender for a non-homicide crime violates the Eighth Amendment's prohibition of cruel and unusual punishment. John Roberts's separate opinion in *Graham* is significant because it rejects a narrow interpretation of the Eighth Amendment — and, more important, the kind of reliance on "original intent" as a method of interpreting the Constitution — that Chief Justice Rehnquist and Justice Scalia espoused.

A fundamental debate about the meaning of the Eighth Amendment is whether it prohibits merely certain methods of punishment, such as disembowelment, or also contains a proportionality requirement that prohibits punishments that are grossly disproportionate to the crime. Because no one questions the fact that a sentence of life without parole is appropriate in some cases, *Graham*, by barring it for some juvenile offenders, reaffirmed that the Eighth Amendment does require that sentences be proportionate.

In his separate opinion, Chief Justice Roberts stated that while he agreed with the result in that case — and thus concurred in the Court's judgment — he disagreed with its decision to announce a categorical rule applicable to all juvenile non-homicide offenses. Instead, he proposed that courts weigh offenders' ages and criminal conduct on a case-by-case basis when determining if sentences violated the Eighth Amendment. In the case at hand, he concluded, the sentence did violate the Eighth Amendment because it contravened the narrow proportionality requirement established in the Court's earlier cases. That position put Roberts directly at odds with his immediate predecessor, Chief Justice Rehnquist, and with Justice Scalia.

In *Harmelin* v. *Michigan,* in 1991, those two justices had been alone in contending that the Eighth Amendment prohibits certain specific kinds of cruel punishments but does not require that the punishment fit the crime. In their view, a life sentence in prison for overtime parking would be constitutional. Justice Scalia recognized that the Court had applied proportionality review only a few years earlier in *Solem* v. *Helm* (1983) (which had overturned as constitutionally disproportionate a repeat offender's sentence to life imprisonment without parole for passing a bad check), but, relying primarily on historical analysis, he announced that "*Solem* was simply wrong." In his view, Justice Powell's opinion for the Court in *Solem* contained two critical flaws: it included only two pages of discussion of the background of the Eighth Amendment, and it had no discussion at all of the understanding of the amendment before the end of the nineteenth century.

Justice Scalia's extensive and interesting discussion of history was based on his own research, rather than the argument advanced by the state, and obviously played a major role in motivating his endorsement of a categorical rule that would prevent judges from considering proportionality when deciding whether a punishment was cruel and unusual. His opinion, however, identifies another factor unrelated to history that was also important to him — the absence of adequate standards for determining when a judge should conclude that a particular sentence is so severe that it violates the Constitution. In his view, the standards discussed by Justice Powell "seem so inadequate that the proportionality principle becomes an invitation to imposition of subjective values."

Justice White disagreed, finding that the text, structure, and purpose of the amendment outweighed Scalia's historical forays. His dissent essentially assumed that Justice Scalia had correctly concluded that the principal reason why the English Declaration of Rights in 1689 and the Eighth Amendment in our Bill of Rights included a prohibition against cruel and unusual punishments was an opposition to particular modes of punishment. But, quoting from an 1832 treatise, White pointed out that the amendment also prohibits "excessive" bail and "excessive" fines, both of which obviously require a determination of proportionality. The treatise noted that in cases in which the judge had discretion both to fine and to imprison a defendant, it would "surely be absurd" to assume his discretion was limited with respect to the amount of the fine but unlimited with respect to the term of imprisonment. I should also mention that the fact that the Eighth Amendment unquestionably imposes a proportionality requirement for bail and for fines without any further limiting standards demonstrates that the framers of the amendment did not share Justice Scalia's concern about permitting judges to exercise discretion based on the facts of individual cases. After all, at a time when most rules of law were the product of common-law adjudication, it was surely appropriate to assume that judges would exercise their discretion wisely.

Justice White's dissent contains a brief quotation from the *Weems* opinion that makes a fundamental point about the relevance of history in constitutional adjudication. In *Weems*, using language that *Harmelin* quoted in part, Justice McKenna observed:

> Legislation, both statutory and constitutional, is enacted, it is true, from an experience of evils but its general language should not, therefore, be necessarily confined to the form that evil had theretofore taken. Time works changes, brings into existence new conditions and purposes. Therefore a principle, to be vital, must be capable of wider application than the mischief which gave it birth. This is peculiarly true of constitutions.

Justice McKenna referred to cases explicating the ex post facto clause and the commerce clause to illustrate his point. I think cases involving two other constitutional provisions even more effectively explain why a narrow focus on the precise evil that gave birth to a constitutional command, even when coupled with contemporary commentary, provides an unreliable guide to understanding the principles enshrined in the Constitution.

At the time of the adoption of the religion clauses in the First Amendment, it was generally believed that they merely proscribed the preference of one Christian faith over another but would not require equal respect for the conscience of the infidel, the atheist, or the adherent of a non-Christian faith such as Islam or Judaism. The commentaries written by Justice Story expressly described this narrow understanding. But as we held in *Wallace v. Jaffree* (1985), "when the underlying principle [was] examined in the crucible of litigation, the Court...unambiguously concluded that the individual freedom of conscience protected by the First Amendment embraces the right to select any religious faith or none at all." And of course, if our construction of the government's duty to rule impartially enshrined in the equal protection clause had been based on contemporary understandings at the time the Fourteenth Amendment was adopted, Thurgood Marshall would have been on the losing side in *Brown* v. *Board of Education*.

As these cases illustrate, reliance on history, even when the interpretation of past events is completely accurate and undisputed, provides an insufficient guide to the meaning of our Constitution. We should also keep in mind that even though we do, and should, rely heavily on the wisdom of individual judges in making countless decisions interpreting and applying rules of law, judges are merely amateur historians. Their interpretations of past events, like their interpretations of legislative history, are often debatable and sometimes simply wrong. Historical analysis is usually relevant and interesting, but it is only one of many guides to sound adjudication.

I cannot finish my discussion of the *Harmelin* case without making these observations about Justice Kennedy's controlling opinion. While he correctly rejected Justice Scalia's extreme view that proportionality has no role to play in the Eighth Amendment analysis, he concluded — quite incorrectly, in Justice White's and my view — that the sentence imposed on Harmelin was permissible. Instead of reviewing why I think it abundantly clear that Justice White had the far better of the argument on the question whether the sentence was constitutionally excessive, I shall merely comment briefly on the historical setting of the opinion.

The justices who joined it were all relatively new occupants of the seats formerly occupied by Justices Stewart, Powell, and Brennan. Based on their votes in earlier Eighth Amendment cases, I am persuaded that all three of those then recently retired justices would have shared Justice White's views in *Harmelin*. Moreover, just as the meaning of the Eighth Amendment itself responds to evolving standards of decency in a maturing society, so also may the views of individual justices become more civilized after twenty years of service on the Court.

Recalling old friends while writing this book has led me to include this one final comment on *Harmelin*. At the beginning of these comments about five chief justices, I referred to my profound admiration for Nat Nathanson. I often think about the wisdom expressed in his repeated admonition to beware of "glittering generalities." The same kind of wisdom was occasionally expressed by Potter Stewart in terse explanations for his vote in cases not easily decided by reference to a bright-line rule. In *Measure for Measure,* one of my favorite Shakespeare plays, Claudio was sentenced to death for having sex with his fiancée before they were officially married. Angelo believed execution of the sentence to be necessary to avoid making a scarecrow of the law. Potter would surely have disagreed. His opinion explaining why the sentence was an act of manifest injustice might have read something like this: "I know it when I see it." Had he had the opportunity to use the same remark to reverse the manifest injustice of Harmelin's life sentence for possessing cocaine in an amount below the carrying capacity of a glove compartment, I would have enthusiastically joined his opinion.

VIII

Second among Equals

Portrait of Judge John Paul Stevens

T HE MOST SENIOR ASSOCIATE Supreme Court justice might reasonably be called the "second among equals." I began to occupy that status when Harry Blackmun retired, in 1994. The duties associated with the position are identical to those performed by every other associate justice, with two exceptions: he or she must sometimes substitute for the chief when the chief is unavailable and also must often assign the preparation of Court opinions when the chief is in dissent.

The unavailability of the chief may result from his disqualification in particular cases, from illness that prevents his participation while he is unable to come to Court, or, of course, from his death. For all three of those reasons, I presided over a significant number of oral arguments and conferences during the final year of Bill Rehnquist's tenure as chief. With one exception, I do not remember that additional responsibility as having made any significant change in the burdens associated with my regular job.

The one exception occurred in January of 2005, when we did not know whether Bill's developing cancer would make it impossible for him to administer the oath of office at the second inauguration of President George W. Bush. Sally Rider, his highly competent administrative assistant, provided me an especially legible copy of the oath and asked me to be prepared to act as a substitute if necessary. On the cold morning of January 20, I memorized the oath and carried a copy in my pocket when all of the members of the Court except for Bill paraded onto the Capitol platform as the national television audience watched. A seat on the platform had been reserved for Bill, but Sally did not yet know whether he would arrive in time to participate. Just moments before the ceremony began, while I was reaching into my pocket to make sure my copy was available, Bill did arrive, and he did administer the oath; he departed promptly after doing so. At the luncheon in the Capitol after the ceremony, President Bush graciously commented on Bill's dedication even though Bill was not present.

President-Elect Barack Obama and Vice President–Elect Joe Biden visit the Supreme Court on January 14, 2009. Pictured in the Justices' Conference Room from left to right: President-Elect Barack Obama, Chief Justice John Roberts, Justices Stevens and Ginsburg, Vice President–Elect Joe Biden, and Justices Souter and Kennedy. *Photograph by Steven Petteway, Collection of the Supreme Court of the United States.*

Justice Stevens administering the oath of office to Vice President–Elect Joe Biden on January 20, 2009. *Photograph by Karen Ballard / Presidential Inaugural Committee.*

Four years later, Joe Biden, who as a senator in 1975 had voted for my confirmation, honored me by asking me to swear him in as vice president. The nine inaugurations that I have attended have all been emotional events. In 1976, when Jimmy Carter replaced Gerald Ford as president, my emotion was a combination of regret that the voters had failed to appreciate Ford's leadership in healing the wounds caused by the Watergate scandal and pride in the fact that the change in power in our great country was being governed by the rule of law. In 2008, the emotion was the jubilation and pride shared by the sea of people stretching from the Capitol to the Lincoln Memorial who were witnessing the inauguration of our first African American president. That it was a glorious day for countless members of both political parties is confirmed by the remarks made by the outgoing President George W. Bush in the Rose Garden after the election:

> No matter how they cast their ballots, all Americans can be proud of the history that was made yesterday. Across the country, citizens voted in large numbers. They showed a watching world the vitality of America's democracy, and the strides we have made toward a more perfect union. They chose a President whose journey represents a triumph of the American story — a testament to hard work, optimism, and faith in the enduring promise of our Nation.

At the inauguration ceremony, before the new president arrived but after most of the invited dignitaries, including George and Laura Bush, had been seated on the platform, Mrs. Obama and her daughters, Malia and Sasha, arrived and greeted the Bushes with real warmth. They had been guests at the White House shortly before, and I had the strong sense that the girls genuinely liked the Bushes and were not just being nice because their parents had told them to be.

I was proud to participate in that momentous event and thought of Bill while doing so.

The only new knowledge that I acquired while presiding at oral arguments is how easy it is for the chief to keep track of the time that remains for the petitioner's lawyer when he or she arises and begins her rebuttal. The chief is always able to give her that information because the marshal meticulously watches the time and has an assistant provide the chief with "time remaining" notes as the argument progresses.

My most significant memory about making assignments of majority opinions when the chief was in dissent is one of satisfaction with a result that I believed to be just. A dissenting judge is never happy, because it is obvious that either the majority has come to the wrong conclusion or his own reasoning is flawed. There are times, however, when a member of the majority may be unhappy about the outcome because he or she may disagree with the result that the law requires. As Thurgood Marshall observed on more than one occasion, the Constitution does not prohibit Congress from enacting stupid laws.

On the relatively few occasions when I had majority opinions to assign, Bill Rehnquist and John Roberts followed the practice of allowing me to make my assignments before they assigned the other majorities. That practice was courteous to me and it also made it easier for them to make an equitable disposition of the other assignments. I seldom, if ever, made an assignment without asking my first choice about his or her willingness to take on the task. And there were few, if any, occasions when my preferred author voiced any objection.

The task of assigning majority opinions is much less burdensome for the "second among equals" than for the chief justice because he or she has relatively few opinions to assign and is not confronted with the need to distribute the work equitably among all nine justices. My principal guideline in making assignments was my judgment about which eligible author would produce the best draft. There were occasions when I kept assignments for myself either because I felt that I had learned some things about a case that I wanted to emphasize in an opinion or because keeping a case or two for myself avoided the risk of receiving a less desirable assignment from the chief. My memory of certain earlier assignments may also have influenced my choice in a few instances.

For example, cases raising First Amendment issues are typically the subject of extensive coverage in the press. I had the impression that Warren Burger would assign the opinions in such cases to himself when the First Amendment claim was vindicated but to Byron White when the opinion would receive a hostile reception on the editorial pages. That practice contributed to Byron's reputation in the press as an enemy of the First Amendment. Because of that history, I tried to avoid assignments that might be interpreted as associating a particular justice with a particular issue.

In cases in which the Court was almost evenly divided, Warren Burger would often assign the opinion to the justice who had the most doubts about the outcome. His reasoning, I believe, was that even if the author changed his mind while drafting the opinion, he would presumably still be able to speak for the Court because the original dissenters would be likely to join his opinion.

I thought that practice wise for a quite different reason. As a practicing lawyer I often began my representation of a client with uncertainty about the validity of his or her position but found that my efforts to justify that position convinced me that it was absolutely right. As a justice there were a few occasions when I changed my mind about the outcome while I was working on the draft of an opinion, but much more frequently I became even more certain that I was right as the drafting process progressed.

In addition to following Warren Burger's example, I also frequently reflected about what I thought at the time was an unwise assignment by Justice Brennan shortly after Justice Kennedy joined the Court. The case of *Patterson* v. *McLean Credit Union* presented us with the question whether racial harassment of Patterson, a black employee, violated a federal statute (42 U.S. Code Section 1981) prohibiting "racial discrimination in the making and enforcement of private contracts." The court of appeals had ruled that conduct that occurred after the contract was formed did not violate the statute. The case was argued twice. At the conference after the first argument, Justice Kennedy voted against Patterson, but the majority decided to have the case reargued to evaluate whether an earlier decision interpreting Section 1981 to apply to private contracts as well as public contracts should be reconsidered. After the second argument, Justice Kennedy changed his mind and was one of the five justices voting in Patterson's favor. Instead of assigning the majority opinion to Justice Kennedy — who obviously had had difficulty with the case — Justice Brennan assigned the opinion to himself. Rather than persuading Justice Kennedy to join, however, the draft must have revived Tony's doubts, for he changed his mind again and ended up writing the majority opinion ruling against Patterson. Congress later overruled that decision by enacting the Civil Rights Reform Act of 1991. Even though Tony might well have written the same unfortunate opinion if Bill had assigned the majority to him, a lesson that I learned while practicing law convinced me that it would have been wiser to ask him to draft the final explanation for his vote at conference.

Occasionally, in the midst of an oral argument, the trial judge will let counsel know that he has made up his mind on an issue in dispute. The lawyer who decides to reinforce the judge's conviction by volunteering an additional argument favoring the result will sometimes be surprised by a response from the judge that he had never considered that point but on reflection finds that it changes his mind about the issue. Hence, the advice that seasoned lawyers have often given to young associates: "Never argue with a judge who is about to rule in your favor." I think that when Bill attempted to provide Tony with additional reasons for adhering to his most recent evaluation of the issues in the Patterson case, he may have overlooked the value of that advice.

I have no memory of regretting any assignment I made, but I do think I hit the nail on the head in at least three important cases (*Blakely* v. *Washington, Romer* v. *Evans,* and *Grutter* v. *Bollinger*) in which the chief was in dissent. Despite the vigorous dissent in each, these three excellent opinions will, I am confident, pass the test of time with flying colors.

In *Blakely* (2004), Justice Scalia wrote a characteristically lucid opinion. That case held that a judge could not impose a more severe sentence than was authorized by the jury's verdict. In response to his four dissenting colleagues, Scalia declared:

> Ultimately, our decision cannot turn on whether or to
> what degree trial by jury impairs the efficiency or fairness

of criminal justice. One can certainly argue that both these values would be better served by leaving justice entirely in the hands of professionals; many nations of the world, particularly those following civil-law traditions, take just that course. There is not one shred of doubt, however, about the Framers' paradigm for criminal justice: not the civil-law ideal of administrative perfection, but the common-law ideal of limited state power accomplished by strict division of authority between judge and jury. As *Apprendi* [v. *New Jersey* (2000)] held, every defendant has the *right* to insist that the prosecutor prove to a jury all facts legally essential to the punishment. Under the dissenters' alternative, he has no such right. That should be the end of the matter.

Perhaps that experience contributed to his claimed entitlement four years later to be "the darling of the criminal defense bar."

Justice Kennedy's opinion for the Court in *Romer* v. *Evans* (1996) — another case in which the chief was in dissent — killed two birds with one missile. First, it invalidated a Colorado statute that treated homosexuals as second-class citizens by, in the words of the Colorado Supreme Court, repealing all existing state and municipal bans on antihomosexual discrimination and "prohibit[ing] any governmental entity from adopting similar, or more protective statutes, regulations, ordinances, or policies in the future." Second, it sounded the death knell to *Bowers* v. *Hardwick,* the 1986 case holding that the due process clause of the Fourteenth Amendment did not forbid Georgia from making it a crime for same-sex couples to engage in conduct that was assumed to be lawful for heterosexuals. By making mere animus toward a group an inadequate rationale for a discriminatory law under the equal protection clause of the Fourteenth Amendment, *Romer* suggested that a criminal prohibition of homosexual sodomy would likely be struck down if challenged on equal protection grounds. Seven years later, in *Lawrence* v. *Texas* (2003), Justice O'Connor took this position. As Justice Kennedy wrote for the majority in that case, *Bowers's* refusal to acknowledge the due process implications of its holding also "sustained serious erosion from...*Romer*." That was one reason that Kennedy was able in *Lawrence* to announce as the opinion of the Court that "*Bowers* v. *Hardwick* should be and now is overruled."

Justice O'Connor convincingly explained — over the chief's dissent — why the University of Michigan Law School's affirmative action program was constitutional in *Grutter* v. *Bollinger* (2003). The decision in that case has an interesting relationship to the president who appointed me to the Court, Gerald Ford.

Ford had long been concerned with fair treatment of minorities when *Grutter* was working its way through the courts. That concern dates at least to his days as a football star at the University of Michigan. One of Ford's good friends and teammates on the 1934 squad was Willis Ward, who happened to be an African American. While that fact would have no special significance today, it was then a matter of critical importance to the Georgia Tech team that was scheduled to visit Ann Arbor to play against Michigan. The visiting team announced that they would boycott the game unless they were assured that Ward would not be allowed to play against them. Gerald Ford was so offended by the ultimatum that he told the coach that he would not play unless Michigan rejected the Georgia demand. Ultimately, however, Ward persuaded him to play because Ward thought it more important to beat Georgia Tech — which Michigan did — than to cancel the game as a protest.

During pendency of the *Grutter* case, Washington, D.C., lawyers Carter Phillips and Virginia Seitz prepared an amicus curiae brief on behalf of a number of senior military officers. A rumor circulated that President Ford played a role in that effort. In response to an inquiry that I made after my retirement, Carter Phillips advised me — while taking pains not to breach any attorney-client privilege — that Ford was both the "but-for" cause of the brief's preparation and filing and the first person to suggest that former military officers as a group had an important message to present to the Court.

On the latter score, Ford's judgment was correct for three reasons. As Justice O'Connor acknowledged in her opinion for the Court, there was a good deal of language in the Court's earlier opinions that suggested that remedying past discrimination was the only permissible justification for race-based governmental action. Rather than discussing any need for — or indeed any interest in — providing a remedy for past sins, the military brief concentrated on describing future benefits that could be obtained from a diverse student body. The authors of the brief did not make the rhetorical blunder of relying on a dissenting opinion to support their legal approach, but they effectively endorsed the views that I had unsuccessfully espoused in an earlier case that involved a black high school teacher in Jackson, Michigan. The Court's holding — that the law school had a compelling interest in attaining a diverse student body—emphasizes the future rather than the past.

The brief also recounted the transition from a segregated to an integrated military. Within a few years of President Truman's 1948 executive order abolishing segregation in the armed forces, the enlisted ranks were fully integrated. Yet during the 1960s and 1970s, they were commanded by an overwhelmingly white officer corps. The chasm between the racial composition of the officer corps and that of the enlisted personnel undermined military effectiveness in a number of ways set forth in the brief. In time, the leaders of the military recognized the critical link between minority officers and military readiness, eventually concluding that "success with the challenge of diversity is critical to national security." They met that challenge by adopting race-conscious recruiting, preparatory, and admissions policies at the service academies and in ROTC programs. The historical discussion in the brief implied that an adverse ruling would jeopardize national security and that an approval of Michigan's programs would provide significant educational benefits for civilian leaders.

The twenty-nine leaders who joined the brief added impressive force to their argument. Fourteen of them — including Wesley Clark and Norman Schwarzkopf—had achieved four-star rank. They were all thoroughly familiar with the dramatic differences between the pre-1948 segregated forces and the modern integrated military. President Ford, who also rendered heroic service during World War II, played a role in selecting them.

Writing for the Court, Justice Sandra Day O'Connor quoted from and embraced this argument from the brief in terms that confirmed the appropriateness of her authorship of the opinion:

At present, "the military cannot achieve an officer corps that is *both* highly qualified *and* racially diverse unless the service academies and the ROTC used limited race-conscious recruiting and admissions policies." ... To fulfill its mission, the military "must be selective in admissions for training and education for the officer corps, *and* it must train and educate a highly qualified, racially diverse officer corps in a racially diverse educational setting." ... We agree that "[i]t requires only a small step from this analysis to conclude that our country's other most selective institutions must remain both diverse and selective." ... Effective participation by members of all racial and ethnic groups in the civil life of our Nation is essential if the dream of one Nation, indivisible, is to be realized. [Bracketing in original.]

Although it was not evident at the time, it is now clear that Gerald Ford shared those views.

Four years ago, in a case involving public school affirmative action programs, Chief Justice John Roberts took a different view, asserting simply, "The way to stop discrimination on the basis of race is to stop discriminating on the basis of race." I am confident that — like the majority of the Court that did not join that part of the chief's opinion — President Ford and the military leaders who filed the amicus brief in *Grutter* would also have declined to concur.

My further comment on my career as the second among equals applies to the entire career of each of the chiefs with whom I served. I have no memory of any member of the Court raising his or her voice during any conference over which I presided or showing any disrespect for a colleague during our discussions. In his State of the Union address in 1976, President Ford eloquently referred to our country as a place where Americans can disagree without being disagreeable. That comment accurately describes the Supreme Court where I worked. It is a place where we not only could but regularly did disagree without being disagreeable.

Epilogue

A s I suggested in my introduction, instead of dividing the history of the Court into seventeen periods, each named for one of the institution's seventeen chief justices, that history might more properly be further subdivided into many more increments, each named after the justice who most recently joined the Court. If so, the precise number of those increments could be the subject of some debate. Most would agree that the original six justices — all appointed in 1789 or 1790 — formed only one new Court. They all participated in their inaugural published decision in 1791. Similarly, Associate Justices Rehnquist and Powell surely marked the introduction of a single new Court, given that they began their service on the same day. A harder question would be presented by two justices who joined the Court on different but nearby dates while the Court continued to do its business, as occurred with Samuel Chase (January 27, 1796) and Oliver Ellsworth (March 4, 1796). However one answers these questions, it was in the most significant case decided during the first term of the Elena Kagan Court that the new second among equals, Justice Scalia, wisely used his assignment authority as the senior justice in the majority to write the Court opinion himself. The case — *Virginia Office for Protection and Advocacy (VOPA)* v. *Stewart* (2011) — arose out of an investigation into the deaths of two patients at state-run mental hospitals. The investigation was conducted by a state agency (VOPA) that received federal funds to advocate and protect the rights of individuals with developmental disabilities. Under the controlling federal statute, VOPA had a right to obtain relevant medical records, but under state law, the officials in charge of the hospitals claimed, those records were privileged. Thus the case raised the novel question whether one state agency (VOPA) claiming that officers of another state agency are violating a federal statute may sue those state officers in a federal court. Over Chief Justice Roberts's dissent, the Court correctly held that the federal court had jurisdiction to require the defendants to obey federal law.

In his characteristically lucid opinion for the Court, Justice Scalia explained that the result followed from a straightforward application of the reasoning in the 1908 decision in *Ex parte Young*. That case held that when a federal court commands a state official to do nothing more than refrain from violating federal law, the official must obey. Because the state cannot empower its officers to violate federal laws in such cases, officers in that circumstance are not agents of the state for sovereign immunity purposes. In his *VOPA* dissent, Chief Justice Roberts argued that if Justice Scalia's interpretation of *Ex parte Young* was correct, "two of our recent precedents were wrongly decided." One of those "recent precedents" was the Rehnquist opinion in *Seminole Tribe* — the roundly criticized case that was primarily responsible for enabling Rehnquist's tenure to set the record for holding the most federal statutes unconstitutional.

Because I firmly believe that the Court's opinion in *Seminole Tribe* will one day be ranked with the majority opinion in the

Lochner case as among the Court's most unfortunate, the debate between Scalia and Roberts is a significant reminder of the need to reexamine that precedent. Their debate is even more significant because both of their opinions are so unequivocal in relying on the interest in protecting the "dignity" of the state as the sole justification for preserving the doctrine of sovereign immunity. The "dignity" rationale for that judge-made doctrine has been repeated over and over again in opinions written after Bill Rehnquist joined the Court. But neither earlier history nor common sense provides any support for the notion that the preservation of a state's "dignity" can justify disobedience of federal law.

In 1821, in his opinion in *Cohens* v. *Virginia* upholding the Supreme Court's appellate jurisdiction in a case in which a state was a defendant, Chief Justice Marshall discussed the history of the Eleventh Amendment. After noting that the amendment was adopted at a time when all the states were greatly indebted and concerned about defending collection claims in federal court, he observed that we must ascribe the amendment "to some other cause than the dignity of a State."

The text of the Constitution does not mention the word *dignity* or the word *sovereignty*. It does, however, state in its preamble that one of its purposes was to "establish Justice." The term *justice* is not defined in either the Constitution itself or in any federal statute of which I am aware. I shall therefore conclude by referring to two quite different ways of thinking about the idea of justice that are both described in Plato's *Republic*.

A serene and elderly gentleman named Cephalus accepted Socrates' suggestion that justice consisted of speaking the truth and paying one's debts, whereas Thrasymachus, a younger and more belligerent antagonist, proclaimed that "justice is nothing more than the interest of the stronger." Presumably the senior citizen would require a ruler to tell the truth and to pay its debts. For Thrasymachus, however, whenever it was in a sovereign's interest to rely on sovereign dignity as a reason for refusing to obey the law, it would be just for him to do so.

An Illinois lawyer named Abraham Lincoln shared Cephalus's thoughts about justice and my views about sovereign immunity. In his State of the Union message of 1861, he said:

> It is as much the duty of Government to render prompt justice against itself, in favor of its citizens, as it is to administer the same between private individuals.

Appendix

CONSTITUTION OF THE UNITED STATES[1]

WE THE PEOPLE of the United States, in Order to form a more perfect Union, establish Justice, insure domestic Tranquility, provide for the common defence, promote the general Welfare, and secure the Blessings of Liberty to ourselves and our Posterity, do ordain and establish this Constitution for the United States of America.

ARTICLE I.

SECTION 1. All legislative Powers herein granted shall be vested in a Congress of the United States, which shall consist of a Senate and House of Representatives.

SECTION 2. [1]The House of Representatives shall be composed of Members chosen every second Year by the People of the several States, and the Electors in each State shall have the Qualifications requisite for Electors of the most numerous Branch of the State Legislature.

[2]No Person shall be a Representative who shall not have attained to the Age of twenty five Years, and been seven Years a Citizen of the United States, and who shall not, when elected, be an Inhabitant of that State in which he shall be chosen.

[3]Representatives and direct Taxes shall be apportioned among the several States which may be included within this Union, according to their respective Numbers, which shall be

---

1 This text of the Constitution follows the engrossed copy signed by Gen. Washington and the deputies from 12 States. The small superior figures preceding the paragraphs designate clauses, and were not in the original and have no reference to footnotes.

determined by adding to the whole Number of free Persons, including those bound to Service for a Term of Years, and excluding Indians not taxed, three fifths of all other Persons.[2] The actual Enumeration shall be made within three Years after the first Meeting of the Congress of the United States, and within every subsequent Term of ten Years, in such Manner as they shall by Law direct. The Number of Representatives shall not exceed one for every thirty Thousand, but each State shall have at Least one Representative; and until such enumeration shall be made, the State of New Hampshire shall be entitled to chuse three, Massachusetts eight, Rhode Island and Providence Plantations one, Connecticut five, New York six, New Jersey four, Pennsylvania eight, Delaware one, Maryland six, Virginia ten, North Carolina five, South Carolina five, and Georgia three.

[4] When vacancies happen in the Representation from any State, the Executive Authority thereof shall issue Writs of Election to fill such Vacancies.

[5] The House of Representatives shall chuse their Speaker and other Officers; and shall have the sole Power of Impeachment.

SECTION 3. [1] The Senate of the United States shall be composed of two Senators from each State, chosen by the Legislature thereof[3] for six Years; and each Senator shall have one Vote.

[2] Immediately after they shall be assembled in Consequence of the first Election, they shall be divided as equally as may be into three Classes. The Seats of the Senators of the first Class shall be vacated at the Expiration of the second Year, of the sec-

---

2 The part of this clause relating to the mode of apportionment of representatives among the several States has been affected by section 2 of amendment XIV, and as to taxes on incomes without apportionment by amendment XVI.

3 This clause has been affected by clause 1 of amendment XVII.

ond Class at the Expiration of the fourth Year, and of the third Class at the Expiration of the sixth Year, so that one third may be chosen every second Year; and if Vacancies happen by Resignation or otherwise, during the Recess of the Legislature of any State, the Executive thereof may make temporary Appointments until the next Meeting of the Legislature, which shall then fill such Vacancies.[4]

[3] No Person shall be a Senator who shall not have attained to the Age of thirty Years, and been nine Years a Citizen of the United States, and who shall not, when elected, be an Inhabitant of that State for which he shall be chosen.

[4] The Vice President of the United States shall be President of the Senate, but shall have no Vote, unless they be equally divided.

[5] The Senate shall chuse their other Officers, and also a President pro tempore, in the Absence of the Vice President, or when he shall exercise the Office of President of the United States.

[6] The Senate shall have the sole Power to try all Impeachments. When sitting for that Purpose, they shall be on Oath or Affirmation. When the President of the United States is tried, the Chief Justice shall preside: And no Person shall be convicted without the Concurrence of two thirds of the Members present.

[7] Judgment in Cases of Impeachment shall not extend further than to removal from Office, and disqualification to hold and enjoy any Office of honor, Trust or Profit under the United States: but the Party convicted shall nevertheless be liable and subject to Indictment, Trial, Judgment and Punishment, according to Law.

SECTION 4. [1] The Times, Places and Manner of holding Elections for Senators and Representatives, shall be prescribed in each

---

4 This clause has been affected by clause 2 of amendment XVIII.

State by the Legislature thereof; but the Congress may at any time by Law make or alter such Regulations, except as to the Places of chusing Senators.

[2] The Congress shall assemble at least once in every Year and such Meeting shall be on the first Monday in December,[5] unless they shall by Law appoint a different Day.

SECTION 5. [1] Each House shall be the Judge of the Elections, Returns and Qualifications of its own Members, and a Majority of each shall constitute a Quorum to do Business; but a smaller Number may adjourn from day to day, and may be authorized to compel the Attendance of absent Members, in such Manner, and under such Penalties as each House may provide.

[2] Each House may determine the Rules of its Proceedings, punish its Members for disorderly Behavior, and, with the Concurrence of two thirds, expel a Member.

[3] Each House shall keep a Journal of its Proceedings, and from time to time publish the same, excepting such Parts as may in their Judgment require Secrecy; and the Yeas and Nays of the Members of either House on any question shall, at the Desire of one fifth of those Present, be entered on the Journal.

[4] Neither House, during the Session of Congress, shall, without the Consent of the other, adjourn for more than three days, nor to any other Place than that in which the two Houses shall be sitting.

SECTION 6. [1] The Senators and Representatives shall receive a Compensation for their Services, to be ascertained by Law, and paid out of the Treasury of the United States.[6] They shall in all Cases, except Treason, Felony and Breach of the Peace, be privi-

---

5 This clause has been affected by amendment XX.
6 This clause has been affected by amendment XXVII.

leged from Arrest during their Attendance at the Session of their respective Houses, and in going to and returning from the same; and for any Speech or Debate in either House, they shall not be questioned in any other Place.

[2] No Senator or Representative shall, during the Time for which he was elected, be appointed to any civil Office under the Authority of the United States, which shall have been created, or the Emoluments whereof shall have been encreased during such time; and no Person holding any Office under the United States, shall be a Member of either House during his Continuance in Office.

SECTION 7. [1] All Bills for raising Revenue shall originate in the House of Representatives; but the Senate may propose or concur with Amendments as on other Bills.

[2] Every Bill which shall have passed the House of Representatives and the Senate, shall, before it become a Law, be presented to the President of the United States; If he approve he shall sign it, but if not he shall return it, with his Objections to that House in which it shall have originated, who shall enter the Objections at large on their Journal, and proceed to reconsider it. If after such Reconsideration two thirds of that House shall agree to pass the Bill, it shall be sent, together with the Objections, to the other House, by which it shall likewise be reconsidered, and if approved by two thirds of that House, it shall become a Law. But in all such Cases the Votes of both Houses shall be determined by Yeas and Nays, and the Names of the Persons voting for and against the Bill shall be entered on the Journal of each House respectively. If any Bill shall not be returned by the President within ten Days (Sundays excepted) after it shall have been presented to him, the Same shall be a Law, in like Manner as if he

had signed it, unless the Congress by their Adjournment prevent its Return, in which Case it shall not be a Law.

[3] Every Order, Resolution, or Vote to which the Concurrence of the Senate and House of Representatives may be necessary (except on a question of Adjournment) shall be presented to the President of the United States; and before the Same shall take Effect, shall be approved by him, or being disapproved by him, shall be repassed by two thirds of the Senate and House of Representatives, according to the Rules and Limitations prescribed in the Case of a Bill.

SECTION 8. [1] The Congress shall have Power To lay and collect Taxes, Duties, Imposts and Excises, to pay the Debts and provide for the common Defence and general Welfare of the United States; but all Duties, Imposts and Excises shall be uniform throughout the United States;

[2] To borrow Money on the credit of the United States;

[3] To regulate Commerce with foreign Nations, and among the several States, and with the Indian Tribes;

[4] To establish a uniform Rule of Naturalization, and uniform Laws on the subject of Bankruptcies throughout the United States;

[5] To coin Money, regulate the Value thereof, and of foreign Coin, and fix the Standard of Weights and Measures;

[6] To provide for the Punishment of counterfeiting the Securities and current Coin of the United States;

[7] To establish Post Offices and post Roads;

[8] To promote the Progress of Science and useful Arts, by securing for limited Times to Authors and Inventors the exclusive Right to their respective Writings and Discoveries;

[9] To constitute Tribunals inferior to the supreme Court;

[10] To define and punish Piracies and Felonies committed on the high Seas, and Offences against the Law of Nations;

[11] To declare War, grant Letters of Marque and Reprisal, and make Rules concerning Captures on Land and Water;

[12] To raise and support Armies, but no Appropriation of Money to that Use shall be for a longer Term than two Years;

[13] To provide and maintain a Navy;

[14] To make Rules for the Government and Regulation of the land and naval Forces;

[15] To provide for calling forth the Militia to execute the Laws of the Union, suppress Insurrections and repel Invasions;

[16] To provide for organizing, arming, and disciplining, the Militia, and for governing such Part of them as may be employed in the Service of the United States, reserving to the States respectively, the Appointment of the Officers, and the Authority of training the Militia according to the discipline prescribed by Congress;

[17] To exercise exclusive Legislation in all Cases whatsoever, over such District (not exceeding ten Miles square) as may, by Cession of particular States, and the Acceptance of Congress, become the Seat of the Government of the United States, and to exercise like Authority over all Places purchased by the Consent of the Legislature of the State in which the Same shall be, for the Erection of Forts, Magazines, Arsenals, dock-Yards, and other needful buildings; — And

[18] To make all Laws which shall be necessary and proper for carrying into Execution the foregoing Powers, and all other Powers vested by this Constitution in the Government of the United States, or in any Department or Officer thereof.

SECTION 9. [1] The Migration or Importation of such Persons as any of the States now existing shall think proper to admit, shall not be prohibited by the Congress prior to the Year one thousand eight hundred and eight, but a Tax or duty may be imposed on such Importation, not exceeding ten dollars for each Person.

[2] The Privilege of the Writ of Habeas Corpus shall not be suspended, unless when in Cases of Rebellion or Invasion the public Safety may require it.

[3] No Bill of Attainder or ex post facto Law shall be passed.

[4] No Capitation, or other direct, Tax shall be laid, unless in Proportion to the Census or Enumeration herein before directed to be taken.[7]

[5] No Tax or Duty shall be laid on Articles exported from any State.

[6] No Preference shall be given by any Regulation of Commerce or Revenue to the Ports of one State over those of another: nor shall Vessels bound to, or from, one State, be obliged to enter, clear, or pay Duties in another.

[7] No Money shall be drawn from the Treasury, but in Consequence of Appropriations made by Law; and a regular Statement and Account of the Receipts and Expenditures of all public Money shall be published from time to time.

[8] No Title of Nobility shall be granted by the United States: And no Person holding any Office of Profit or Trust under them, shall, without the Consent of the Congress, accept of any present, Emolument, Office, or Title, of any kind whatever, from any King, Prince, or foreign State.

---

7 This clause has been affected by amendment XVI.

SECTION 10. [1] No State shall enter into any Treaty, Alliance, or Confederation; grant Letters of Marque and Reprisal; coin Money; emit Bills of Credit; make any Thing but gold and silver Coin a Tender in Payment of Debts; pass any Bill of Attainder, ex post facto Law, or Law impairing the Obligation of Contracts, or grant any Title of Nobility.

[2] No State shall, without the Consent of the Congress, lay any Imposts or Duties on Imports or Exports, except what may be absolutely necessary for executing its inspection Laws: and the net Produce of all Duties and Imposts, laid by any State on Imports or Exports, shall be for the Use of the Treasury of the United States; and all such Laws shall be subject to the Revision and Control of the Congress.

[3] No State shall, without the Consent of Congress, lay any Duty of Tonnage, keep Troops, or Ships of War in time of Peace, enter into any Agreement or Compact with another State, or with a foreign Power, or engage in War, unless actually invaded, or in such imminent Danger as will not admit of delay.

ARTICLE II.

SECTION 1. [1] The executive Power shall be vested in a President of the United States of America. He shall hold his Office during the Term of four Years, and, together with the Vice President, chosen for the same Term, be elected, as follows

[2] Each State shall appoint, in such Manner as the Legislature thereof may direct, a Number of Electors, equal to the whole Number of Senators and Representatives to which the State may be entitled in the Congress: but no Senator or Representative, or

Person holding an Office of Trust or Profit under the United States, shall be appointed an Elector.

[3] The Electors shall meet in their respective States, and vote by Ballot for two Persons, of whom one at least shall not be an Inhabitant of the same State with themselves. And they shall make a List of all the Persons voted for, and of the Number of Votes for each; which List they shall sign and certify, and transmit sealed to the Seat of the Government of the United States, directed to the President of the Senate. The President of the Senate shall, in the Presence of the Senate and House of Representatives, open all the Certificates, and the Votes shall then be counted. The Person having the greatest Number of Votes shall be the President, if such Number be a Majority of the whole Number of Electors appointed; and if there be more than one who have such Majority, and have an equal Number of Votes, then the House of Representatives shall immediately chuse by Ballot one of them for President; and if no Person have a Majority, then from the five highest on the List the said House shall in like Manner chuse the President. But in chusing the President, the Votes shall be taken by States, the Representation from each State having one Vote; A quorum for this Purpose shall consist of a Member or Members from two thirds of the States, and a Majority of all the States shall be necessary to a Choice. In every Case, after the Choice of the President, the Person having the greatest Number of Votes of the Electors shall be the Vice President. But if there should remain two or more who have equal Votes, the Senate shall chuse from them by Ballot the Vice President.[8]

---

8 This clause has been superseded by amendment XII.

[4] The Congress may determine the Time of chusing the Electors, and the Day on which they shall give their Votes; which Day shall be the same throughout the United States.

[5] No Person except a natural born Citizen, or a Citizen of the United States, at the time of the Adoption of this Constitution, shall be eligible to the Office of President; neither shall any Person be eligible to that Office who shall not have attained to the Age of thirty five Years, and been fourteen Years a Resident within the United States.

[6] In Case of the Removal of the President from Office, or of his Death, Resignation, or Inability to discharge the Powers and Duties of the said Office,[9] the Same shall devolve on the Vice President, and the Congress may by Law provide for the Case of Removal, Death, Resignation or Inability, both of the President and Vice President, declaring what Officer shall then act as President, and such Officer shall act accordingly, until the Disability be removed, or a President shall be elected.

[7] The President shall, at stated Times, receive for his Services, a Compensation, which shall neither be encreased nor diminished during the Period for which he shall have been elected, and he shall not receive within that Period any other Emolument from the United States, or any of them.

[8] Before he enter on the Execution of his Office, he shall take the following Oath or Affirmation: — "I do solemnly swear (or affirm) that I will faithfully execute the Office of President of the United States, and will to the best of my Ability, preserve, protect and defend the Constitution of the United States."

SECTION 2. [1] The President shall be Commander in Chief of

---

9 This clause has been affected by amendment XXV.

the Army and Navy of the United States, and of the Militia of the several States, when called into the actual Service of the United States; he may require the Opinion, in writing, of the principal Officer in each of the executive Departments, upon any Subject relating to the Duties of their respective Offices, and he shall have Power to grant Reprieves and Pardons for Offences against the United States, except in Cases of Impeachment.

[2] He shall have Power, by and with the Advice and Consent of the Senate, to make Treaties, provided two thirds of the Senators present concur; and he shall nominate, and by and with the Advice and Consent of the Senate, shall appoint Ambassadors, other public Ministers and Consuls, Judges of the supreme Court, and all other Officers of the United States, whose Appointments are not herein otherwise provided for, and which shall be established by Law: but the Congress may by Law vest the Appointment of such inferior Officers, as they think proper, in the President alone, in the Courts of Law, or in the Heads of Departments.

[3] The President shall have Power to fill up all Vacancies that may happen during the Recess of the Senate, by granting Commissions which shall expire at the End of their next Session.

SECTION 3. He shall from time to time give to the Congress Information of the State of the Union, and recommend to their Consideration such Measures as he shall judge necessary and expedient; he may, on extraordinary Occasions, convene both Houses, or either of them, and in Case of Disagreement between them, with Respect to the Time of Adjournment, he may adjourn them to such Time as he shall think proper; he shall receive Ambassadors and other public Ministers; he shall take Care that the Laws be faithfully executed, and shall Commission all the Officers of the United States.

SECTION 4. The President, Vice President and all civil Officers of the United States, shall be removed from Office on Impeachment for, and Conviction of, Treason, Bribery, or other high Crimes and Misdemeanors.

ARTICLE III.

SECTION 1. The judicial Power of the United States, shall be vested in one supreme Court, and in such inferior Courts as the Congress may from time to time ordain and establish. The Judges, both of the supreme and inferior Courts, shall hold their Offices during good Behaviour, and shall, at stated Times, receive for their Services, a Compensation, which shall not be diminished during their Continuance in Office.

SECTION 2. [1] The judicial Power shall extend to all Cases, in Law and Equity, arising under this Constitution, the Laws of the United States, and Treaties made, or which shall be made, under their Authority; — to all Cases affecting Ambassadors, other public Ministers and Consuls; — to all Cases of admiralty and maritime Jurisdiction; — to Controversies to which the United States will be a party; — to Controversies between two or more States; — between a State and Citizens of another State;[10] — between Citizens of different States, — between Citizens of the same State claiming Lands under Grants of different States, and between a State, or the Citizens thereof, and foreign States, Citizens or Subjects.

[2] In all Cases affecting Ambassadors, other public Ministers

---

10 This clause has been affected by amendment XI.

and Consuls, and those in which a State shall be Party, the supreme Court shall have original Jurisdiction. In all the other Cases before mentioned, the supreme Court shall have appellate Jurisdiction, both as to Law and Fact, with such Exceptions, and under such Regulations as the Congress shall make.

[3] The Trial of all Crimes, except in Cases of Impeachment, shall be by Jury; and such Trial shall be held in the State where the said Crimes shall have been committed; but when not committed within any State, the Trial shall be at such Place or Places as the Congress may by Law have directed.

SECTION 3. [1] Treason against the United States, shall consist only in levying War against them, or in adhering to their Enemies, giving them Aid and Comfort. No Person shall be convicted of Treason unless on the Testimony of two Witnesses to the same overt Act, or on Confession in open Court.

[2] The Congress shall have Power to declare the Punishment of Treason, but no Attainder of Treason shall work Corruption of Blood, or Forfeiture except during the Life of the Person attainted.

ARTICLE IV.

SECTION 1. Full Faith and Credit shall be given in each State to the public Acts, Records, and judicial Proceedings of every other State. And the Congress may by general Laws prescribe the Manner in which such Acts, Records and Proceedings shall be proved, and the Effect thereof.

SECTION 2. [1] The Citizens of each State shall be entitled to all Privileges and Immunities of Citizens in the several States.

[2] A Person charged in any State with Treason, Felony, or other Crime, who shall flee from Justice, and be found in another State, shall on Demand of the executive Authority of the State from which he fled, be delivered up, to be removed to the State having Jurisdiction of the Crime.

[3] No Person held to Service or Labour in one State, under the Laws thereof, escaping into another, shall, in Consequence of any Law or Regulation therein, be discharged from such Service or Labour, but shall be delivered up on Claim of the Party to whom such Service or Labour may be due.[11]

SECTION 3. [1] New States may be admitted by the Congress into this Union; but no new State shall be formed or erected within the Jurisdiction of any other State; nor any State be formed by the Junction of two or more States, or Parts of States, without the Consent of the Legislatures of the States concerned as well as of the Congress.

[2] The Congress shall have Power to dispose of and make all needful Rules and Regulations respecting the Territory or other Property belonging to the United States; and nothing in this Constitution shall be so construed as to Prejudice any Claims of the United States, or of any particular State.

SECTION 4. The United States shall guarantee to every State in this Union a Republican Form of Government, and shall protect each of them against Invasion; and on Application of the Legislature, or of the Executive (when the Legislature cannot be convened) against domestic Violence.

---

11 This clause has been affected by amendment XIII.

ARTICLE V.

The Congress, whenever two thirds of both Houses shall deem it necessary, shall propose Amendments to this Constitution, or, on the Application of the Legislatures of two thirds of the several States, shall call a Convention for proposing Amendments, which, in either Case, shall be valid to all Intents and Purposes, as Part of this Constitution, when ratified by the Legislatures of three fourths of the several States, or by Conventions in three fourths thereof, as the one or the other Mode of Ratification may be proposed by the Congress; Provided that no Amendment which may be made prior to the Year One thousand eight hundred and eight shall in any Manner affect the first and fourth Clauses in the Ninth Section of the first Article; and that no State, without its Consent, shall be deprived of its equal Suffrage in the Senate.

ARTICLE VI.

[1]All Debts contracted and Engagements entered into, before the Adoption of this Constitution, shall be as valid against the United States under this Constitution, as under the Confederation.

[2]This Constitution, and the Laws of the United States which shall be made in Pursuance thereof; and all Treaties made, or which shall be made, under the Authority of the United States, shall be the supreme Law of the Land; and the Judges in every State shall be bound thereby, any Thing in the Constitution or Laws of any State to the Contrary notwithstanding.

[3]The Senators and Representatives before mentioned, and the Members of the several State Legislatures, and all executive and

judicial Officers, both of the United States and of the several States, shall be bound by Oath or Affirmation, to support this Constitution; but no religious Test shall ever be required as a Qualification to any Office or public Trust under the United States.

ARTICLE VII.

The Ratification of the Conventions of nine States, shall be sufficient for the Establishment of this Constitution between the States so ratifying the Same.

DONE in Convention by the Unanimous Consent of the States present the Seventeenth Day of September in the Year of our Lord one thousand seven hundred and Eighty seven and of the Independence of the United States of America the Twelfth

IN WITNESS whereof We have hereunto subscribed our Names,

G⁰. WASHINGTON — Presidᵗ.
and deputy from Virginia

[Signed also by the deputies of twelve States.]

Delaware

Geo: Read, Gunning Bedford Jun, John Dickinson, Richard Bassett, Jaco: Broom

Maryland

James McHenry, Dan of St Thos Jenifer, Danl Carroll

Virginia

John Blair, James Madison Jr.

North Carolina

Wm Blount, Rich^d. Dobbs Spaight, Hu Williamson

South Carolina

J. Rutledge, Charles Cotesworth Pinckney, Charles Pinckney, Pierce Butler

Georgia

William Few, Abr Baldwin

New Hampshire

John Langdon, Nicholas Gilman

Massachusetts

Nathaniel Gorham, Rufus King

Connecticut

W^m. Saml. Johnson, Roger Sherman

New York

Alexander Hamilton

New Jersey

Wil: Livingston, David Brearley, W^m. Paterson, Jona: Dayton

Pennsylvania

B Franklin, Thomas Mifflin, Robt Morris,
Geo. Clymer, Thos. Fitzsimons, Jared Ingersoll, James
Wilson, Gouv Morris

Attest: William Jackson *Secretary*

Articles in addition to, and Amendment of, the Constitution of the United States of America, proposed by Congress, and ratified by the Legislatures of the several states, pursuant to the fifth Article of the original Constitution

ARTICLE [I.]¹²

Congress shall make no law respecting an establishment of religion, or prohibiting the free exercise thereof; or abridging the freedom of speech, or of the press; of the right of the people peaceably to assemble, and to petition the Government for a redress of grievances.

ARTICLE [II.]

A well regulated Militia, being necessary to the security of a free State, the right of the people to keep and bear Arms, shall not be infringed.

ARTICLE [III.]

No Soldier shall, in time of peace be quartered in any house, without the consent of the Owner, nor in time of war, but in a manner to be prescribed by law.

ARTICLE [IV.]

The right of the people to be secure in their persons, houses, papers, and effects, against unreasonable searches and seizures, shall not be violated, and no Warrants shall issue, but upon probable cause, supported by Oath or affirmation, and particularly

---

12 Only the 13th, 14th, 15th, and 16th articles of amendment had numbers assigned to them at the time of ratification.

describing the place to be searched, and the persons or things to be seized.

ARTICLE [V.]

No person shall be held to answer for a capital, or otherwise infamous crime, unless on a presentment or indictment of a Grand Jury, except in cases arising in the land or naval forces, or in the Militia, when in actual service in time of War or public danger; nor shall any person be subject for the same offence to be twice put in jeopardy of life or limb; nor shall be compelled in any criminal case to be a witness against himself, nor be deprived of life, liberty, or property, without due process of law; nor shall private property be taken for public use, without just compensation.

ARTICLE [VI.]

In all criminal prosecutions, the accused shall enjoy the right to a speedy and public trial, by an impartial jury of the State and district wherein the crime shall have been committed, which district shall have been previously ascertained by law, and to be informed of the nature and cause of the accusation; to be confronted with the witnesses against him; to have compulsory process for obtaining witnesses in his favor, and to have the Assistance of Counsel for his defense.

ARTICLE [VII.]

In Suits at common law, where the value in controversy shall exceed twenty dollars, the right of trial by jury shall be preserved, and no fact tried by a jury, shall be otherwise re-examined in any

Court of the United States, than according to the rules of the common law.

ARTICLE [VIII.]

Excessive bail shall not be required, nor excessive fines imposed, nor cruel and unusual punishments inflicted.

ARTICLE [IX.]

The enumeration in the Constitution, of certain rights, shall not be construed to deny or disparage others retained by the people.

ARTICLE [X.]

The powers not delegated to the United States by the Constitution, nor prohibited by it to the States, are reserved to the States respectively, or to the people.

ARTICLE [XI.]

The Judicial power of the United States shall not be construed to extend to any suit in law or equity, commenced or prosecuted against one of the United States by Citizens of another State, or by Citizens or Subjects of any Foreign State.

ARTICLE [XII.]

The Electors shall meet in their respective states, and vote by ballot for President and Vice-President, one of whom, at least, shall not be an inhabitant of the same state with themselves; they shall name in their ballots the person voted for as President, and in distinct ballots the person voted for as Vice-President, and they shall make distinct lists of all persons voted for as President, and of all persons voted for as Vice-President, and of the number of votes for each, which lists they shall sign and certify, and transmit sealed to the seat of the government of the United States, directed to the President of the Senate; — The President of the Senate shall, in the presence of the Senate and House of Representatives, open all the certificates and the votes shall then be counted; — The person having the greatest number of votes for President, shall be the President, if such number be a majority of the whole number of Electors appointed; and if no person have such majority, then from the persons having the highest numbers not exceeding three on the list of those voted for as President, the House of Representatives shall choose immediately, by ballot, the President. But in choosing the President, the votes shall be taken by states, the representation from each state having one vote; a quorum for this purpose shall consist of a member or members from two-thirds of the states, and a majority of all the states shall be necessary to a choice. And if the House of Representatives shall not choose a President whenever the right of choice shall devolve upon them, before the fourth day of March next following, then the Vice-President shall act as President, as in the case of the death or other constitutional disability of the President.[13] — The person having the greatest number of votes as Vice-President, shall be the Vice-President, if such number be a majority of the whole number of Electors appointed, and if no person have a majority, then from the two highest numbers on the list, the Senate shall choose the Vice-President; a quorum for the purpose shall consist of two-thirds of the whole number of

13 This sentence has been superseded by section 3 of amendment XX.

Senators, and a majority of the whole number shall be necessary to a choice. But no person constitutionally ineligible to the office of President shall be eligible to that of Vice-President of the United States.

ARTICLE XIII.

SECTION 1. Neither slavery nor involuntary servitude, except as a punishment for crime whereof the party shall have been duly convicted, shall exist within the United States, or any place subject to their jurisdiction.

SECTION 2. Congress shall have power to enforce this article by appropriate legislation.

ARTICLE XIV.

SECTION 1. All persons born or naturalized in the United States, and subject to the jurisdiction thereof, are citizens of the United States and of the State wherein they reside. No State shall make or enforce any law which shall abridge the privileges or immunities of citizens of the United States; nor shall any State deprive any person of life, liberty, or property, without due process of law; nor deny to any person within its jurisdiction the equal protection of the laws.

SECTION 2. Representatives shall be apportioned among the several States according to their respective numbers, counting the whole number of persons in each State, excluding Indians not taxed. But when the right to vote at any election for the choice of electors for President and Vice President of the United States, Representatives in Congress, the Executive and Judicial officers of a State, or the members of the Legislature thereof, is denied to any of the male inhabitants of such State, being twenty-one years of age,[14] and citizens of the United States, or in any way abridged, except for participation in rebellion, or other crime, the basis of representation therein shall be reduced in the proportion which the number of such male citizens shall bear to the whole number of male citizens twenty-one years of age in such State.

SECTION 3. No person shall be a Senator or Representative in Congress, or elector of President and Vice President, or hold any office, civil or military, under the United States, or under any State, who, having previously taken an oath, as a member of Congress, or as an officer of the United States, or as a member of any State legislature, or as an executive or judicial officer of any State, to support the Constitution of the United States, shall have engaged in insurrection or rebellion against the same, or given aid or comfort to the enemies thereof. But Congress may by a vote of two-thirds of each House, remove such disability.

SECTION 4. The validity of the public debt of the United States, authorized by law, including debts incurred for payment of pensions and bounties for services in suppressing insurrection or rebellion, shall not be questioned. But neither the United States nor any State shall assume or pay any debt or obligation incurred in aid of insurrection or rebellion against the United States, or any claim for the loss or emancipation of any slave; but all such debts, obligations and claims shall be held illegal and void.

SECTION 5. The Congress shall have power to enforce, by appropriate legislation, the provisions of this article.

---

14 See amendment XIX and section 1 of amendment XXVI.

ARTICLE XV.

SECTION 1. The right of citizens of the United States to vote shall not be denied or abridged by the United States or by any State on account of race, color, or previous condition of servitude.

SECTION 2. The Congress shall have power to enforce this article by appropriate legislation.

ARTICLE XVI.

The Congress shall have power to lay and collect taxes on incomes, from whatever source derived, without apportionment among the several States, and without regard to any census or enumeration.

ARTICLE [XVII.]

The Senate of the United States shall be composed of two Senators from each State, elected by the people thereof, for six years; and each Senator shall have one vote. The electors in each State shall have the qualifications requisite for electors of the most numerous branch of the State legislatures.

When vacancies happen in the representation of any State in the Senate, the executive authority of such State shall issue writs of election to fill such vacancies: Provided, That the legislature of any State may empower the executive thereof to make temporary appointments until the people fill the vacancies by election as the legislature may direct.

This amendment shall not be so construed as to affect the election or term of any Senator chosen before it becomes valid as part of the Constitution.

ARTICLE [XVIII.][15]

SECTION 1. After one year from the ratification of this article the manufacture, sale, or transportation of intoxicating liquors within, the importation thereof into, or the exportation thereof from the United States and all territory subject to the jurisdiction thereof for beverage purposes is hereby prohibited.

SECTION 2. The Congress and the several States shall have concurrent power to enforce this article by appropriate legislation.

SECTION 3. This article shall be inoperative unless it shall have been ratified as an amendment to the Constitution by the legislatures of the several States, as provided in the Constitution, within seven years from the date of the submission hereof to the States by the Congress.

ARTICLE [XIX.]

The right of citizens of the United States to vote shall not be denied or abridged by the United States or by any State on account of sex.

Congress shall have power to enforce this article by appropriate legislation.

ARTICLE [XX.]

SECTION 1. The terms of the President and Vice President shall end at noon on the 20th day of January, and the terms of Senators and Representatives at noon on the 3d day of January, of the years in which such terms would have ended if this article had

---

15 Repealed by section 1 of amendment XXI.

not been ratified; and the terms of their successors shall then begin.

SECTION 2. The Congress shall assemble at least once in every year, and such meeting shall begin at noon on the 3d day of January, unless they shall by law appoint a different day.

SECTION 3. If, at the time fixed for the beginning of the term of the President, the President elect shall have died, the Vice President elect shall become President. If a President shall not have been chosen before the time fixed for the beginning of his term, or if the President elect shall have failed to qualify, then the Vice President elect shall act as President until a President shall have qualified; and the Congress may by law provide for the case wherein neither a President elect nor a Vice President elect shall have qualified, declaring who shall then act as President, or the manner in which one who is to act shall be selected, and such person shall act accordingly until a President or Vice President shall have qualified.

SECTION 4. The Congress may by law provide for the case of the death of any of the persons from whom the House of Representatives may choose a President whenever the right of choice shall have devolved upon them, and for the case of the death of any of the persons from whom the Senate may choose a Vice President whenever the right of choice shall have devolved upon them.

SECTION 5. Sections 1 and 2 shall take effect on the 15th day of October following the ratification of this article.

SECTION 6. This article shall be inoperative unless it shall have been ratified as an amendment to the Constitution by the legislatures of three-fourths of the several States within seven years from the date of its submission.

ARTICLE [XXI.]

SECTION 1. The eighteenth article of amendment to the Constitution of the United States is hereby repealed.

SECTION 2. The transportation or importation into any State, Territory, or possession of the United States for delivery or use therein of intoxicating liquors, in violation of the laws thereof, is hereby prohibited.

SECTION 3. This article shall be inoperative unless it shall have been ratified as an amendment to the Constitution by conventions in the several States, as provided in the Constitution, within seven years from the date of the submission hereof to the States by the Congress.

ARTICLE [XXII.]

SECTION 1. No person shall be elected to the office of the President more than twice, and no person who has held the office of President, or acted as President, for more than two years of a term of which some other person was elected President shall be elected to the office of the President more than once. But this Article shall not apply to any person holding the office of President when this Article was proposed by the Congress, and shall not prevent any person who may be holding the office of President, or acting as President, during the term within which this Article becomes operative from holding the office of President or acting as President during the remainder of such term.

SECTION 2. This article shall be inoperative unless it shall have been ratified as an amendment to the Constitution by the legislatures of three-fourths of the several States within seven years from the date of its submission to the States by the Congress.

ARTICLE [XXIII.]

SECTION 1. The District constituting the seat of Government of the United States shall appoint in such manner as the Congress may direct:

A number of electors of President and Vice President equal to the whole number of Senators and Representatives in Congress to which the District would be entitled if it were a State, but in no event more than the least populous State; they shall be in addition to those appointed by the States, but they shall be considered, for the purposes of the election of President and Vice President, to be electors appointed by a State; and they shall meet in the District and perform such duties as provided by the twelfth article of amendment.

SECTION 2. The Congress shall have power to enforce this article by appropriate legislation.

ARTICLE [XXIV.]

SECTION 1. The right of citizens of the United States to vote in any primary or other election for President or Vice President, for electors for President or Vice President, or for Senator or Representative in Congress, shall not be denied or abridged by the United States or any State by reason of failure to pay any poll tax or other tax.

SECTION 2. The Congress shall have power to enforce this article by appropriate legislation.

ARTICLE [XXV.]

SECTION 1. In case of the removal of the President from office or of his death or resignation, the Vice President shall become President.

SECTION 2. Whenever there is a vacancy in the office of the Vice President, the President shall nominate a Vice President who shall take office upon confirmation by a majority vote of both Houses of Congress.

SECTION 3. Whenever the President transmits to the President pro tempore of the Senate and the Speaker of the House of Representatives his written declaration that he is unable to discharge the powers and duties of his office, and until he transmits to them a written declaration to the contrary, such powers and duties shall be discharged by the Vice President as Acting President.

SECTION 4. Whenever the Vice President and a majority of either the principal officers of the executive departments or of such other body as Congress may by law provide, transmit to the President pro tempore of the Senate and the Speaker of the House of Representatives their written declaration that the President is unable to discharge the powers and duties of his office, the Vice President shall immediately assume the powers and duties of the office as Acting President.

Thereafter, when the President transmits to the President pro tempore of the Senate and the Speaker of the House of Representatives his written declaration that no inability exists, he shall resume the powers and duties of his office unless the Vice President and a majority of either the principal officers of the executive department[16] or of such other body as Congress may by law provide, transmit within four days to the President pro tempore of the Senate and the Speaker of the House of Representatives their written declaration that the President is unable to discharge the powers and duties of his office. Thereupon Congress shall decide the issue, assembling within forty-eight hours for that purpose if not in session. If the Congress, within twenty-one days after receipt of the latter written declaration, or, if Congress is not in session, within twenty-one days after Congress is required to assemble, determines by two-thirds vote of both Houses that the President is unable to discharge the powers and duties of his office, the Vice President shall continue to discharge the same as Acting President; otherwise, the President shall resume the powers and duties of his office.

ARTICLE [XXVI.]

SECTION 1. The right of citizens of the United States, who are eighteen years of age or older, to vote shall not be denied or abridged by the United States or by any State on account of age.

SECTION 2. The Congress shall have power to enforce this article by appropriate legislation.

ARTICLE [XXVII.]

No law, varying the compensation for the services of the Senators and Representatives, shall take effect, until an election of Representatives shall have intervened.

---

16 So in original. Probably should be "departments."

Acknowledgments

One pleasure of writing this book was getting to work with old friends and valued colleagues. Another is the opportunity to recognize their contributions in print. Some come readily to mind — my classmate and contemporary Art Seder (we were born on the same day), who clerked for Fred Vinson; my former law partner, the late Ed Rothschild, who counseled me during my confirmation hearings; Judge Tim Dyk of the United States Court of Appeals for the Federal Circuit and Frank Beytagh, former Dean of the Moritz College of Law at the Ohio State University, both former clerks for Earl Warren; and countless present and former employees of the Supreme Court. Bill Suter, the incomparable Clerk of the Court, for example, is not just the source of statistical data but also the man who measured the distance between the lectern and the chief justice for me. And Catherine Fitts, the curator, verified the history of the statue of John Marshall. At the Library of Congress, Daun Van Ee has facilitated important research for the book. As was true with respect to the many judicial opinions I have written over the years, I have received invaluable help from my law clerk Sam Erman throughout my work on this book; from his successor, Dina Mishra, with its conclusion; and from library assistants Linda Corbelli, Jill Duffy, Patricia Evans, Michelle Humphries, Melissa Kreiling, Linda Maslow, Catherine Romano, Sara Sonet, and Kate Wilko.

ACKNOWLEDGMENTS

I am grateful to Peter Edwards, my aide to chambers, for his ongoing logistical efforts. My agent, Peter Bernstein; my editor, Geoff Shandler; and Geoff's staff at Little, Brown and Company suggested important improvements and deserve praise for helping shepherd this project to completion. With the help of Steve Petteway, the Court photographer, the pictures in the volume were selected by my secretary, Janice Harley, and by my beautiful dietician, who happens to be married to me.

Index

Page numbers in *italics* refer to photographs

Index

About the Author

John Paul Stevens received a bachelor's degree in English literature from the University of Chicago. On December 6, 1941, he joined the Navy and spent most of World War II at Pearl Harbor, analyzing Japanese naval communications. Afterward, he studied law at Northwestern University and was then employed as a law clerk for Justice Wiley Rutledge of the U.S. Supreme Court during its 1947–48 term. He practiced law in Chicago from 1949 until 1970, when President Nixon nominated him to be a judge on the United States Court of Appeals for the Seventh Circuit. In addition to building a private practice before becoming a judge, Stevens served as associate counsel to the Subcommittee on the Study of Monopoly Power of the House Judiciary Committee (1951–52), as a member of the National Committee to Study the Antitrust Laws (1953–54) appointed by Attorney General Herbert Brownell, and as general counsel (1967) to a special commission that was investigating the integrity of a judgment of the Illinois Supreme Court and that resulted in the resignation of two members of that court. He was also active in the work of the Chicago Bar Association, having been elected second vice president shortly before leaving private practice to become a judge.

In 1975, President Ford nominated Stevens to become the

101st Justice of the United States Supreme Court, where he served until his retirement in 2010. Now a father, grandfather, and great-grandfather, Stevens, with his wife, splits his time between the District of Columbia and Florida. He continues to write and speak about the Court.